J. Powell

SUCCESSFUL SCHOOL IMPROVEMENT

MODERN EDUCATIONAL THOUGHT
Series Editor: Professor Andy Hargreaves,
            Ontario Institute for Studies in Education

This important new series contains some of the very best of modern educational thought that will stimulate interest and controversy among teachers and educationalists alike.

It brings together writers of distinction and originality within educational studies who have made significant contributions to policy and practice. The writers are all scholars of international standing who are recognized authorities in their own particular field and who are still actively researching and advancing knowledge in that field.

The series represents some of their best and most distinctive writing as a set of provocative, interrelated essays addressing a specific theme of contemporary importance. A unique feature of the series is that each collection includes a critical introduction to the author's work written by another influential figure in the field.

Current titles:

Roger Dale: *The State and Education Policy*
Michael G. Fullan: *Successful School Improvement*
Jane Gaskell: *Gender Matters from School to Work*
Andy Hargreaves: *Curriculum and Assessment Reform*
Martyn Hammersley: *Classroom Ethnography*
Jean Rudduck: *Innovation and Change*

Successful School Improvement

The Implementation Perspective and Beyond

MICHAEL G. FULLAN

OPEN UNIVERSITY PRESS
Buckingham · Philadelphia

Open University Press
Celtic Court
22 Ballmoor
Buckingham
MK18 1XW

and

1900 Frost Road, Suite 101
Bristol, PA 19007, USA

First published 1992

A catalogue record of this book is available
from the British Library

Library of Congress Cataloging-in-Publication Data

Fullan, Michael.
    Successful school improvement: the implementation perspective and
beyond / Michael G. Fullan.
        p.   cm.
    Includes bibliographical references (p.) and index.
    ISBN 0-335-09576-3 — ISBN 0-335-09575-5 (pbk.)
        1. School improvement programs.   2. Education—Data processing.
3. Curriculum enrichment.   4. Teachers—Training of.   5. Educational
change.   I. Title.
LB2822.8.F85   1992
371.2—dc20   91-44338
                                                                                CIP

Typeset by Inforum Typesetting, Portsmouth
Printed in Great Britain by St Edmundsbury Press, Bury St Edmunds

Contents

Preface

Educational change fails many more times than it succeeds. One of the main reasons is that implementation – or the process of achieving something new into practice – has been neglected. During the 1970s and 1980s a number of us have been working on a 'practical theory of change', attempting to uncover the many layers of complexity in the change process. This book is an attempt to convey some of the things we have learned in using the implementation perspective for successful school improvement. Chapter 1 provides an overview of this knowledge, identifying factors and processes associated with success, and pointing to courses of action.

The remaining chapters are more specific but no less fundamental. Chapter 2 investigates the implementation issues involved in the use of microcomputers in classrooms – a highly popular but complex innovation of the 1980s and 1990s. Chapter 3 shifts attention to the school district in a case study of a school district model for systematic curriculum implementation. Chapter 4 takes a fresh look at the pivotal role of the school principal as a leader of institutional development and reform.

Chapter 5 clarifies the role of staff development and innovation. Since staff development is widely regarded as critical for implementation, it is important to sort out its role, which is indeed powerful, but multifaceted. This chapter links staff development with fundamental school improvement. The final chapter takes up the issue of how teacher development, school development and implementation are interrelated. The limitations of the concept of implementation are examined, while taking up more basic issues of teacher and institutional development needed for lasting school improvement.

I have been fortunate to work directly with the best international experts in implementation over the years. I learned a great deal and made many friendships. I acknowledge with gratitude what I have learned and enjoyed, in working with the following colleagues: Stephen Anderson, Barrie Bennett, Ray Bolam, Michael Connelly, David Crandall, Per Dalin, Peter Grimmett, Gene Hall, Andy Hargreaves, David Hopkins, Michael Huberman, Bruce

Joyce, Pierre Laderriere, Ken Leithwood, Judith Little, Karen Louis, Susan Loucks-Horsley, Milbrey McLaughlin, Matt Miles, Earle Newton, Paul Park, Carol Rolheiser-Bennett, Seymour Sarason, Geoff Scott, Suzie Stiegelbauer, Dennis Thiessen, Rein van der Vegt, Nancy Watson and Marv Wideen. I would especially like to thank Andy Hargreaves for suggesting and sponsoring the present book, and Michael Huberman for his fine and substantial introduction. It is an honour to be associated with these colleagues.

Finally my gratitude, ever more frequently recently, to Dolora Harvey, who typed the manuscript with the usual alacrity and accuracy.

Critical Introduction

MICHAEL HUBERMAN

Opening remarks: on the pleasure of writing critical introductions

Putting aside the time and labour required, it is usually a pleasure to write an introduction to a book. First of all, one normally writes them for books one likes, and for authors whose work one respects. The authors themselves, of course, are generally careful to make sure this is the case before asking, but you never know. With fellow specialists on school improvement as friends, sometimes you don't need enemies. This is especially the case with 'critical introductions' – like this one.

It is also a pleasure to write introductions because it allows the commentator to sift through a fellow specialist's work and to highlight as 'essential' the very themes he agrees with the most or on which his own work has centred. The reader will soon find me doing precisely this, when arguing that this book tells us several new things about the change process since the field was last reviewed comprehensively.

Finally, writing an introduction to this book will enable me to raise some questions which, in my opinion, are answered here in other ways than the ways I would have addressed them. Some of them are questions with which I will be taking issue with the author. But most are ones which no one has resolved completely when actually coming to grips with the implementation of significant instructional changes in schools, be it change on a one-shot or on a continuous basis. The pleasure here is less that of giving the impression that one knows more or better than the author – unless the critic actually believes this – than of being able to pinpoint some interesting points without the burden of having to work them through. Introductions, after all, are just that, and the reader is impatient to get to the substance of the book itself.

With this list of pleasurable tasks, I have mapped the terrain for the remainder of this text. First, I shall try to put Michael Fullan's work in perspective and, from that vantage point, assess his contribution to our understanding of the change process and its management. Then, I shall take up one or two general issues raised in this book and try to show how they capture both the promise and the perils of enacting significant change in schools. From here, I shall move on to the several, more particular themes that represent for me a more intricate understanding of the dynamics at work when new programmes and practices or new organizational arrangements are brought into schools or designed there. And, finally, I shall address a few topics with which I shall try to seduce the reader into complementary ways of looking at the same phenomena.

Towards a 'social technology' of school improvement

Since the early 1970s Michael Fullan has been a major figure, both conceptually and practically, in the field of educational change and improvement. For professionals and fellow researchers in this field, the author's periodic reviews of research on the implementation of innovations have made him into an authoritative 'chronicler' of the field. This is not an easy status to achieve. Literally thousands of articles and dozens of books are written each year on 'school improvement'. Many of them are read, some with interest. A very small number of these are re-read and cited ritually in more recent publications. They become the social scientist's equivalent of 'classics': texts from which newcomers invariably reap more information and enlightenment than they can take in the first time through – they will typically underline three-quarters of the article or book; texts which veterans to the field re-read with delight, often marvelling at the new insights they missed the last time through. The insights were often missed incidentally, because these professionals simply hadn't 'seen' these insights previously and thus discovered them only after another cycle of experience and reflection on their work.

It is remarkable that Michael Fullan has produced or co-produced at least three such pieces: a seminal review of the 'change' literature (Fullan and Pomfret 1977), a book synthesizing this and the more recent work in the field (*The Meaning of Educational Change*) in 1982 and, in 1991, another comprehensive synthesis (*The New Meaning of Educational Change*). In the most recent 'classic', we have, in fact, more than a synthesis: something close to a reframing of the field, complete with an 'agenda' both for researchers and for practitioners at grips with the actual implementation of discrete changes or with ways of sustaining institutional cultures that appear to promote continuous self-inquiry, professional interaction and experimentation.

The present volume is essentially a case study version of the *New Meaning*. It also provides more 'case' material and more 'prescriptive' material. That is it illustrates the main findings from recent empirical research and translates them into suggestions for ongoing policy and practice. It takes us from the data to their meaning, then to the possible levers of action. It gets us there quickly, perhaps even a bit *too* quickly. In fact, I would argue that readers of this book would do well to work their way through the *New Meaning* before springing immediately into action on the strength of the recommendations made or inferred here. To understand, for example, how the 'complexity' of an innovation actually affects adoption, initial use and technical mastery in the classroom, calls for our understanding what complexity 'is' in different types and contexts of use, why too little of it is self-defeating but too much of it is overwhelming, and how it interacts with other important factors one should be keeping in mind. Or to understand why we have moved from 'tight' planning to a more 'rolling', evolutionary model of the change process requires more space and some conceptual archeology beyond the scope of this text. Or again: to read, as a principal, that it is important to 'hold users accountable for the change' and, at the same time, to give wide 'latitude for errors' may appear bewildering without understanding precisely what this means, how the two precepts are conciliable and at which point in the process one may be more important than the other. In other words, the author has taken some shortcuts here, in large part to make readers' work easier, and I am arguing for readers to take a *vademecum* along with them in order not to get into mischief.

The shortcuts are all the shorter because of two other virtues in Michael Fullan's work: its comprehensiveness and its accessibility. Most researchers in the field of educational change pick out a small patch to cultivate, and seldom venture far afield. Even within that small patch, in fact, they remain snugly within the bounds of the scientific community. Anyone else is asking for trouble. Speaking personally, as someone who asks for trouble – who tries to move regularly from the study of educational change to actual attempts to enact instructional changes in school systems or to advise others over the life of the project – I am *still* uncomfortable at other levels than at the classroom level, or with other lenses than those of a psychologist or social psychologist.

What the author does, here and elsewhere, is to enumerate and intertwine the multiple levels at which the change process operates. In many chapters of this text, we go between the district office, the community, the school building, the principal's office, the classroom or project centre, even into the heads of individual teachers and pupils. In social scientific terms, we are trying to bridge constructs and findings from political science, sociology social psychology and psychology, not to mention cognate fields and not to get into the matter of which sub-field or line of inquiry of, say, social psychology we are contending with. And we are doing it by integrating information *from* the field – from the empirical study of change – rather than by plastering those constructs on the multi-layered process we are trying to illuminate.

This is no small task and no small contribution. It puts much of the knowledge base in one place, overcoming the usual fragmentation of a field of study. No professional, in effect, can *afford* to look at the change process from only one perspective, or she will be run over from behind. It frames the issues in terms of 'contexts' (e.g. school buildings, district offices) and readily understandable factors (e.g. 'continuous assistance') rather than in terms of constructs or variables. Unlike much of the general or comprehensive literature on innovation, it avoids homilies and war stories, thereby staying 'honest' by confronting its conclusions with findings from empirical research. And within that body of research, Fullan exercises some fairly rigorous quality control, such that we are not getting studies that selectively support one view of the process or of its determinants. To do all this in under 200 pages is, as the French say, a *tour de force*, but it does mean an economy of explication and nuance and, here and there, sets a pace that can leave a novice to the field fairly breathless.

All the same, a student of the change process can find in one place – here, or in the *New Meaning* – both a digest of what is understood about the change process at different levels and a compelling account of how these levels may actually affect one another in the course of adoption, implementation or what has come to be known as the 'institutionalization' of change.

If we take this text, along with the successive string of syntheses and perspectives drawn from Fullan's other work, do we have a 'handbook' for the planning and implementation of educational change? No. We may, in fact, never have one. Or, if we do come up with one, it may not override changes in the ways we think schools should perform or even changes in the emerging configurations of schools and instructional practices. Or if it does override those changes, it will be in the form of a model of such abstraction that it will provide no local guidance.

We are, however, much closer than before to an understanding of many of the dynamics at work. We know far better what to expect at each 'layer' of an educational enterprise and each stage of the change process. We are surprised far less often by what happens, and can account for it more completely once it has happened. We even know how and, more important, why certain factors or their combination tend to produce certain effects – why, for example, administrative 'pressure and support' can be a powerful tandem for sustaining innovations that involve significant changes in day-to-day instructional practice in the classroom. We cannot, however, predict when 'pressure' or 'support' or both are appropriate in a case we have not yet encountered, nor know in advance which form either or both should take. Nor are we likely to get there anytime soon. For one thing, we have studied those factors and their effects in too few settings. For another thing, there are just too many moving parts.

So Fullan's work tells us, to a large extent, what to expect: where we are in this field of study, what we know about implementation, what that knowledge means, and how it may usefully serve as a guide to enacting and sustaining significant change in schools. It also tells us what we do not know. And it may be more profitably used, I think, as a guide than as a handbook – as a sourcebook for educating interested professionals about the change process, its determinants, and about some promising avenues for 'moving' school districts, buildings or classrooms from one constellation to another, more desirable one.

A damnedly complicated business

That we can now assemble some of the pieces of a 'soft technology' for implementing educational change is an important step forward. It has, in fact, been an arduous process, with some radiant moments of acceleration from work done by North Americans such as Michael Fullan, Matt Miles, Ron

Havelock and Ken Leithwood, along with their European counterparts. It is also desperately important work, at least in my eyes. Obviously, the quality and degree of pupils' learning, motivation and development are at stake in any major attempt to change instructional practices. Beyond this, however, is the fact that we have apparently managed our affairs poorly up to now.

Consider an example. Michael Fullan refers in this text to our work in Switzerland on teachers' professional life-cycles: how teachers traverse thirty-five to forty years of life and work in the classroom; which changes in self-perceptions, relationships, levels of commitment, instructional concerns and mastery and the like are undergone at different stages of the career trajectory; what 'professional satisfaction' means in the teaching profession and under which conditions it is actually achieved – or not.

One of the clearest findings in that study – and in its replications in other countries – was that teachers progressively 'focused' their work and their energies at the classroom level, and disengaged from participation in multiple-classroom changes or more 'systemic' changes at the building or district levels. Like Voltaire's Candide, after his series of misadventures, the older teachers 'cultivated their gardens', figuratively speaking, and built protective walls around them. Within those bounds – with the preferred pupils, assignments, schedules, streams, programmes and classrooms they had acquired by dint of seniority – they tinkered with bits of their curriculum or modes of evaluation or activity formats. More precisely, the most *satisfied* teachers tinkered, and the others either disinvested more seriously or essentially went through the annual motions. Their reaction to larger-scale changes, recent or remote ones, was either whimsical or hostile. In virtually all cases, however, they were severe judges of what they variously described as botched, chaotic, exhausting or cynical projects or reforms in which they had invested heavily – usually with pleasure and oftentimes with enthusiasm. From their perspective, as people who had stayed in the classroom and observed the longer-term effects of curriculum, structural or instructional reforms, the game had not been worth the candle. This in contrast to ex-colleagues who had 'ridden' the reforms to administrative or political promotions. The most dissatisfied teachers, in fact, were those who had invested the most in these structural reforms.

Put crudely, informants felt that implementation had been mismanaged – some even talked about 'betrayal' – and mismanaged in many of the ways the author illustrates in this text. More subtly, however, they were saying that 'cultivating their gardens' was a deliberate choice to limit their universe to changing things they could control – to bits and pieces of their annual pro-gramme or of their instructional repertoire. At this level, at least, things turned out predictably or, if not, the surprises were manageable and sometimes enrich-ing ones, and the whole process was not too exhausting. By contrast, at the cross-classroom or the cross-school level, programme innovation was, at best, a lottery, even for those administrators who presumably had the power and resources to control the course of events.

On the face of it, this is a severe indictment of the implementation of educational change. It suggests either that the process is typically, even chronically, mismanaged or that, beyond a certain level of complexity or ambition, it is fundamentally unmanageable. Or some combination of the two.

This means in turn that a better understanding of implementation is bound to reduce the casualty rate, but that there may also be limits to what we can actually 'deliver' at any given site with any given project. The reasons are legion, but a few are worth mentioning. The too-many-moving-parts problem means that there will be unanticipated events continuously using up the time set aside for managing the innovation. One may then get into a mode of reacting to circumstances and never get to the point of anticipating or determining them. The more complex the change – the greater number of parts, of actors, of changes required in working arrangements, curriculum components, instructional practices, training and assistance devices – the greater the chance of internal turbulence.

Without internal turbulence, on the other hand, without some minimal levels of complexity, we are essentially wasting our time with trivia. Or, more precisely, we are all too likely to take potentially important changes and gradually turn them into trivia, as we go from one half-measure to another, in the name of operational or interpersonal tranquility. If we have learned one thing in the 'school improvement' game, in fact, it is that certain forms of pain and disorder are healthy signs. They indicate that a system is changing intrinsically and, with it, that we have increased the chances of actually achieving *other* outcomes than the ones we have typically obtained, i.e. the ones we were dissatisfied with in the first place. We will probably not have these problems if we replace the chalk in the classroom or the microscopes in the biology lab. But if we take out the chalk and the blackboards to work more with manipulative, group-based maths activities, or if we combine lab work with field visits to collect a variety of micro-organisms, and we do all this in forty-five schools in which 85 per cent of the teachers involved had never dreamed of reorganizing their fall trimester [autumn term] in this way, we can expect, very quickly, some 'promising' pain and disorder.

We come out, then, with intriguing paradoxes. That smooth initial implementation is usually a sign of trivial change. That problems of initial sacrifices *elsewhere* (less time for mathematics, more confusing transitions or scheduling, contradictory evaluation criteria) are in fact signs that significant changes are being enacted. That rapid success can lead, very quickly, to rapid decline (key people leave or turn their attention elsewhere, replaced by others with lesser credentials or another agenda). That there is no necessary relationship between the proven success of an innovation – even in terms of increments in pupils' achievement or capacities – and its longevity. We could come back the following year and it will have disappeared from sight. That when principals or school district administrators feel 'ownership' of an innovation, which is to the good, they tend to create coteries, and then to treat those outside these coteries as 'resisters' or 'foot-draggers' (or worse), which then actually produces genuine resisters and foot-draggers at the point of implementation. Such paradoxes abound, and they draw our attention to the intricacies of managing change in schools.

Added to this is the fact that we are always at the mercy of external turbulence: budget cuts, personnel shifts, restructuring the latest management scheme from the private sector, feverish parent campaigns and the like. And the fact that the introduction of significant change at the point of actual application, in the classroom, increases the level of teachers' uncertainties and, thereby, lowers the threshold at which these uncertainties will trigger the more irrational, emotional aspects of institutional life that are always just below the surface. 'Managing' change then becomes a matter of containing irrational behaviour, whereas we had assumed we were embarked on a rational process of achieving desirable objectives. Such behaviour, in this instance, often takes the form of unsettled interpersonal accounts which, at the first serious signs of stress or apparent failure, can create a climate of defensiveness that soon dissolves into bickering, outbursts, slammed doors and intermittent bursts of reconciliation and new divorces.

So implementation is a tricky business, even in the best of times. We are trying to change people's professional lives, while at the same time changing their stable working arrangements. We are doing it with practices unproven in this immediate context and in the name of outcomes we are not sure we can actually achieve. And we are ministering to minors – pupils – which is always ethically delicate and politically hazardous. These pupils, moreover, will usually prefer living with the devils they know than those being dangled in front of them, and can therefore exert a mostly conservative, braking influence. And, when it comes to resistance to change, they have literally made a career of opportunistic dissimulation that can fool the wisest of practitioners.

These are some of the reasons why Michael Fullan's work is important. It may also explain why, near the end, he shows less interest in the implementation of distinct innovations than in the creation of a greater institutional *capacity* to innovate: to diagnose problems before they have become crises, to seize opportunities during the brief moments they are there (i.e. typically paid for by someone else), to generate temporary mechanisms and resources for critical support functions and, more generally, to manage moments of change as routinely as one manages moments of stability.

The problem here, as Fullan explains well, is that it takes several cycles of trial and error, of collective reflection on the process, of honing the component parts of the process, of accumulated skill in managing both the technical and social-emotional aspects of change, of choosing the appropriate level of ambition and the correct pace of change, etc., for such a capacity to take root. 'Capacity' does not come off the shelf from the local supermarket. When we visit schools with these qualities, just as when we visit exceptional teachers or exceptional administrators or exceptional pupils, we assume the change process is a straightforward one. We don't see the automatisms at work and we only see a few of the strings being pulled. If we then return to our own, inexperienced environment and try to replicate what we have seen, all hell breaks loose. This does not mean that more conservative or 'novice' institutions will necessarily find it harder to enact changes, but that first, the 'social technology' will need to be different, and second, the course of actual events will be more uncertain.

Every change is a process of grafting the new on to the old, and every 'old' is a distinctive, local context with its own history and configuration.

Some insights from *Successful School Improvement*

At the outset, I promised to identify some meaningful themes in this book. I confessed that the choice of themes would be arbitrary and narcissistic: themes which I regard, perhaps narrowly, as emerging, important developments in the field, and themes from my own recent work. Notice that I have separated the two propositions.

A new, 'phenomenological' focus

It is always intriguing when a sociologist, like Michael Fullan, insists on the importance of the *meaning* of change to those involved in its adoption and implementation. It has long been assumed in the 'school improvement' field that well-designed programmes or projects would find their way easily into school environments, where professionals could rationally weigh their merits. We know better now. Significant changes have virtually no reality outside of what local actors think they are: why they are changes, whether they are desirable ones, how difficult they will be to execute, how well they 'fit' with the regnant teaching or organizational styles in the building. We are in the realm of perceptions, even in the most technological or materials-based projects, and these perceptions will determine the actions, or inactions, that follow. That these meanings are different across actors and that they will necessarily evolve over time does not make our work any easier. But we would be foolish to ignore them or to weigh them less seriously than the more instrumental aspects of changing an instructional programme or resolving a core institutional problem.

What Fullan also underscores in this regard is that perceptions are often a function of the phenomenal world in which actors are living and that, as a result, the administrator's world may be very different from the teacher's world. An illustration: many studies show that teachers chronically underestimate the difficulty of making organizational changes and administrators chronically underestimate the complexities of changing classroom-level practices. If those administrative underestimates translate, for example, into fewer resources, less training, greater impatience, heavier criticism – as they often do – we may have compromised the chances of successful use. On the one hand, we have planful direction, long-term perspectives, identifiable constraints, tangible accountability, separation of issues or tasks into managerially distinct chunks, interactions with adults. In the classroom, on the other hand, we have relational denseness, continuous improvisation, simultaneous and tangled management of events and children, mysterious or even unfathomable shifts in pupils level of interest and activity, short-term objectives (getting through the lesson, the chapter, the morning).

That these universes are perceived differently, that objectives deemed important in one are seen as incidental in another, that people self-select in and out of each universe and then seldom 'visit' one another thereafter: all these things mean that proposed changes, along with the vehicles for implementing them, are usually not construed in the same way, without either side being aware of the fact. The greatest problems arise when the administrative or policy level gets 'unhooked' from events at the point of application: in the classroom or in the resource room, or in the project centre. Without continuous monitoring of what is happening locally, we sail off, very quickly, into Wonderland. Teachers are then often obliged to feed selective, self-protective information to administrators who are now transmitting good news to the outside world and cannot contend with bad news from within.

Evolutionary, 'rolling' models of change

Here, too, perspectives on implementation have shifted. Initially, we had conceived of 'planned change' as an elaborate, 'up front' exercise of marshalling resources, training key practitioners, mapping out strategies in advance and setting timelines for the introduction of more complex components. We have now learned that the resources, the training, the strategies, the timelines are all forms of liquidity, which we would be better to spend as we go, leaving as much slack as we can for monitoring where we have come from and anticipating what is around the next corner.

In many ways, the school of 'cognitive behaviourists' had it right: we actually find out who we are when we watch ourselves act and what we think when we hear ourselves saying something. So it is with the implementation of change: we need to act in order to create the context for reflection on what our next acts should be. The action itself will qualitatively change the situation in ways that can tell us how to plan. At the same time, we will be at another place, cognitively speaking, than we were before we took the next step. And, *a fortiori*, at a very different place than we would have been if we have done all our planning in advance – committing our resources, freezing ourselves into sequences and timelines that will turn out to have been unrealistic and will then get in our way – by imagining what the most desirable course of events would be. The metaphor is not the orchestra, with its methodological rehearsals, but rather the jazz group, improvising continuously within the bounds of implicit understandings, even rituals, among its members about melodic progression.

Achieved clarity, achieved commitment

Here, many of us analysts of the change process have been durably influenced by the work of social psychologists in the tradition of Kurt Lewin. We have believed, for example, that if people participate early on in the process of designing school-level changes, they will develop 'ownership' of the project and, at the same time, will have a clearer sense of what the components of the project actually entail.

The dynamics of the particular case of school settings turn out to be more complex, for some of the reasons mentioned earlier. As Michael Fullan points out, Matt Miles and I found out in *Innovations Up Close* that teachers developed commitment to the changes under study only as they began to master them in the classroom (Huberman and Miles 1984). It was the experience of increasing skill in delivering and varying the programmes, along with the attendant headiness of actually obtaining results one had thought beyond one's reach, that produced ownership. Before then, commitment to the project was a fragile, fundamentally mercurial commodity. It could evaporate after a rotten week or a stormy meeting. Similarly, understanding of the purposes, premises, mechanics and materials of the project, and of the relationships between these several components, was initially fuzzy and undifferentiated. It was only when teachers had undergone a few cycles of experimentation, then reflected on what appeared to be emerging 'constants' and began toying with different combinations of them, that they got on top of the programme in conceptual terms. This, in turn, strengthened their technical mastery and heightened their commitment.

As Fullan shows, this same pattern is beginning to emerge from other empirical work. It also confirms more experimental work in cognitive and social psychology. This is heartening. The main point, however, is that it calls for our rethinking the design of implementation, for example, by putting most of our initial chips on the achievement of technical mastery (through assistance, through exchange, through the facilitation of institutional constraints), rather than on trying to assure that, cognitively and politically, everyone is on board at the beginning.

Outcomes – getting to the end of the chain

As Michael Fullan points out, school improvement was once considered 'done' when a new programme or practice was decided upon. It was as if adopting a practice were tantamount to its actually being put in practice. Through some pioneering work in programme evaluation, most notably by Gene Hall and Susan Loucks (1977), we discovered that when we compared these 'innovations' with 'conventional practices', we were making some magical assumptions, and should have known better. Many of these 'innovations' had not taken place. Worse still, some of the 'conventional practices' had actually turned into implementations of our 'innovations'.

This then led to an emphasis on the actual *implementation* of change, to be sure that the changes had occurred and that, having occurred, they bore at least a family resemblance to what we had had in mind at the outset. Or, if not, that they had, at the least, not turned into monstrosities. One never knows. Researchers then took up the issue of *institutionalization*. Innovations that have been implemented need longevity to have any durable effects, and assuring such longevity is a more artful affair than one had imagined. As noted earlier, proven and acknowledged success is usually a necessary but by no means a sufficient requirement for institutionalization. Our research, along with Robert Yin's has shown that, under certain conditions, dismal projects can be institutionalized and highly successful ones can be buried (Huberman and Miles 1984; Yin *et al.* 1984).

But let us stay for a moment with these 'durable effects'. It is only recently, very recently, that we have looked more closely at outcomes beyond the successful implantation of the change itself. In fact, we are still focusing more attention on effects at the teacher level than at the pupil level. Many of these data are of questionable reliability; they have to do with teachers' self-reported changes in behaviour or attitude or in professional capacity more broadly. But even more robust studies that independently testify to greater explicitness or awareness or instructional versatility on the part of teachers, as a result of a major change in instructional practice, are slightly beside the point. Putting it crudely, innovations are not introduced to improve professional capacity; they are introduced to heighten pupils' skills and capacities. True, we are not likely to get the second without the first, but by getting different instruction, we may not necessarily get more learning. And if we settle for the 'teacher capacity' outcome, we are, in subtle ways, distracting ourselves from the reasons for which we made the change in the first place.

Michael Fullan does well, then, to attract our attention to what the Americans call, not very felicitously, the 'bottom line' of the balance sheet, and to draw on studies that can actually demonstrate the causal relationship between adoption → implementation → enhanced technical capacity → revised institutional arrangements → measurable impacts on pupils in line with the 'thrust' of the innovation. Without that causal chain, we shall have no 'social technology' of implementation. Nor shall we be able to talk about 'school improvement' with a straight face. And by not addressing the impact on pupils, we will have indulged in the same magical thinking as before: that adoption meant implementation . . . that implementation meant institutionalization . . . that enhanced teacher capacity means enhanced pupil achievement or development.

These relationships are not, of course, linear ones. And an overly obsessive concern with 'impact data' will invariably lead to reliance on meaningless or problematic indicators (e.g. residualized gain scores on standardized achievement tests – oftentimes to measure innovations that are not about achievement gains in the first place). Still, if changes in organizational and instructional practices are not followed down to the level of effects on pupils, we will have to admit more openly that we are essentially investing in staff development rather than in the improvement of pupils' abilities.

In fact, even if we strive for the larger objective – the enhancement of institutional 'capacity' via an internal process of continuous diagnosis, experimentation, exchange within the school building – we are still not out of the woods. It still remains to be shown that greater institution-level capacities actually deliver more benefits to pupils than does, let us say, a fragmented teaching staff that has few diagnostic mechanisms, few professional interactions, few norms of continuous improvement, a benign but lethargic principal, and so on. The empirical evidence is thinner here than one might assume, perhaps because the relationship seems so intuitively obvious – or so desirable.

But is it so obvious? In low-income, urban settings, with energetic, intrusive principals, such institutional capacities seem to make a difference in the achievement levels of pupils. Elsewhere, the evidence is far more equivocal. In effect, whenever we move from the institutional level to the classroom, we are not only shifting contexts but also shifting the ground rules by which people can or will follow through on agreements made elsewhere. And then, when we go from enhanced instructional capacity in the classroom to actual changes in pupils' conduct or attitudes, we have another transactional shift whose alchemy is far more complex than we often let on.

Innovation and staff development

Not that staff development and, beyond that, enhanced professional capacity are unworthy components of educational change. As it happens, these are often crucial by-products that may not occur otherwise. Innovations mobilize people – administrators, teachers, pupils – to change their practices where otherwise they would probably have hedged their bets: done nothing, or done less.

The case is clearest with external innovations – ones for which schools and/ or school staff are the 'targets' rather than the initiators of the co-elaborators. If, as a teacher, you have no necessary 'stake' in the change being visited on you, why do it? In our studies, the initial answer has been clear: 'because I have no choice'. (Within that 'no choice', of course, are a multitude of choices, but more on that point in a moment.) The next answers are more intriguing ones: 'because I can get some new materials' . . . 'because I can experiment in my class and with my colleagues on school time' . . . 'because I can get some free in-service training right in line with what is going on in my classroom' . . . 'because I can get access to first-class consultants I'd never get to work with otherwise' . . . 'because it's time I tried something else, and this will make me change some things I had been putting off for years now'. In other words, these innovations were essentially pretexts for enhanced professional development. And the *form* in which that development occurred – close to one's everyday practice, close to one's peers, with tailored training and assistance, in continuous cycles of experimentation and reflection – tells us a lot about how, ideally, conventional in-service offerings should be put together, and seldom are.

In the same vein, when we study the outcomes of these innovations, be they externally or locally derived, we can observe changes in instructional philosophies, strategies, materials, routines and capacities that go well beyond the introduction or modification of a particular programme within the school. Many of these outcomes are 'second-order' effects, in the form of new awareness, new understandings, new skills that typically transfer to other tasks or to other sectors than the ones contingent on the original project. So the implementation of change can be a powerful vehicle for the improvement of professional capacity, above and beyond the scope or the effects of the innovation itself.

The collective implementation of change can have other fruitful by-products. For example, there is evidence that teachers, much like other artists and artisans, typically stay away from one another's workshops. Within the school building, one does not ask spontaneously for help and one does not cavalierly offer advice. Both behaviours are reckless. To ask for help is publicly to compromise one's professional reputation (self-abasement); to offer help is to violate important norms of status equality (arrogance, hubris, bad form). One may ask for help *indirectly*, by telling a story about a period wasted on a diabolical pupil or an unrepentant class or an extraordinary morning that went inexplicably sour in the afternoon. And one can offer advice, indirectly, by 'telling back' a story that contains some germs of resolution, but with all the necessary qualifiers ('Of course, if I had *your* group, it probably wouldn't have worked out').

In the process of enacting significant changes, these norms often change. Since everyone is in over her head, no one is expected to perform well. Since we are all learning, making mistakes, finding solutions serendipitously, it is all right to ask for help and to give advice – much like a field trip, when the children leave behind half the picnic on the train and it rains and the museum is closed for repairs. I will never forget the remark of a teacher in one of our field studies of educational change who said, with respect to her colleague next door, 'Before this, we had nothing to do with one another. Now it's as if I have a helper when I get into trouble. She has me and I have her.'

In sum, implementation creates interdependencies between members of an institution – as much between administrators and teachers as between teachers – who, up to then, had carefully organized their work so as to be as free as possible of the effects of others on the accomplishment of their core tasks. On an institutional level, this can be the beginning of more general changes – in climate, in collaboration, in collective responsibility for the career of pupils – that, here again, transcend any particular innovation. More often than not, however, this does not happen. The process of implementation remains a singular event in the life history of the school: memorable, significant, not without lingering effects on relationships and working arrangements. But the former norms reassert themselves gradually, depressing once again both the level and the quality of professional interactions.

The unevenness of technical mastery

In my own work, I have concentrated on the ways in which teachers come to understand and master new instructional approaches and practices. As Michael Fullan points out, we now know that this is a slow, uneven process, filled with plateaux, regressions and moments of real distress. For some of our readers, *Innovation Up Close* (Huberman and Miles 1984) is a litany of woes, especially in the sections having to do with initial implementation. Later on in the process, fortunately, there is invariably more celebrating.

We are coming to understand better *why* technical mastery is so difficult to achieve and, more important, what kinds of assistance are useful at which stage of the process. As I said earlier, we also know better what kinds of distress and which regressions are in fact fruitful, change-bearing ones, and how best they can be endured without succumbing to the temptation of 'down-sizing' the project, or of 'pausing' or breaking it into 'more manageable bits'. Because this, in fact, is what typically happens. The classroom, for example, is a crowded, quicksilver place, and it functions smoothly because a fairly complex set of routines have been implicitly agreed upon and 'grooved'. Many of those routines have to do with instructional materials and sequences which lend predictability and, much of the time, productivity to the daily cycle. Innovations of any magnitude – ones worth investing heavily in – are inherently disruptive. Above all, they consume important amounts of teachers' energies with very low initial yields in instructional efficiency. Cutting back and slowing down are adaptive responses. For several reasons, however, they seldom give rise, later on, to restoring the cuts and speeding up the pace. Typically, studies of innovation 'mastery' on the part of teachers show that, up to two or three years after adoption, most have either reduced the scale of the project or are still operating with the most rudimentary components. When that happens of course, we are not likely to see the 'impacts' everyone has banked on – especially the administrators.

This is one of the reasons why intelligent combinations of 'pressure' and 'support' may be the best ticket. But it takes a cunning administrator to concoct the right mixture at the right time, and to use it differentially on his staff. Too much pressure is bullying; too much support actually suggests to teachers that they will need crutches for years on end.

Two metaphors may help here. Imagine that you are learning to drive, on your third time out with your instructor. She says, 'Now I want you to go down this hill and in 200 metres shift down to second gear, because you will be turning right half a kilometre later. So remember to look in your rear-view mirror and, after you have shifted, put on your turn signal.'

It is likely that 80 per cent of cognitive space available to you is mobilized by the simple task of staying on the road and avoiding the cars in front and behind you. Preparing for down-shifting is already consuming the other 20 per cent and, when you actually do it, will eat heavily into the 80 per cent you needed to survey the road. The rear-view mirror, the turn signal: these are luxuries you feel you will never, ever be able to integrate into your driving. This is what the initial stages of technical mastery feel like. They give us precious indications about how much information teachers can process, what kinds of assistance are appropriate, and what the increments in complexity should be.

If that support is provided and our neophyte driver stays with his lessons at the same level of demandingness, he will quickly forget his early tribulations. We will find him three years later, driving to work, simultaneously down-shifting, braking, putting on his turn signal and changing lanes, while at the same time changing the radio station. And, perhaps even in parallel, ruminating on his schedule for the morning – that is, not *thinking* about the several simultaneous operations he is conducting on the road. Having 'automatized' those procedures, he is free, cognitively speaking, to work on more complex problems – just as the teacher who has achieved a high level of technical mastery is now in the process of making important changes in the innovation in order to get more consequential results. This is what the later stages of technical mastery are about, and they dictate another pattern of assistance (e.g. observations of more experienced peers and experts, more technical exchanges, more conceptually demanding forms of training).

In both cases, incidentally, assistance which includes real-time, within-the-classroom observation, demonstration and coaching on the part of outsiders is likely to speed up the process. This is another important point made in this book. Drawing incisively on the work of Bruce Joyce and Beverly Showers (1988), whose work has often been distorted, Fullan insists on the fact that novice innovators need 'hands-on' tutoring just as much as novice skiers or gymnasts need it. Mastery of complex instructional programmes or sequences is not done best, or even well, by lone wolves experimenting through trial and error in their classrooms, no matter how experienced those wolves may be. Aside from the waste involved, the bad habits developed, the resulting missunderstandings of the new programme and its components, the auto-didactics of implementation do not result in viable, professional levels of mastery. The training and coaching have to occur not only outside the classroom, but inside as well. They may even be as indispensable as they are intrusive.

This, of course, is heretical talk. 'What, me, with fifteen years of teaching biology under my belt, one of the "master" teachers in this district, I am going to let myself be "coached" by some "expert" – maybe even by another biology teacher whom no one knows around here – in my own classroom?' The answer is: yes, you'd be a fool not to. It's precisely what you do in every other sector of your life when you try to learn a particularly demanding, complex new set of skills, from building a cabin to taking an advanced degree. Saying that, however, wreaks havoc with professional norms. In effect, privacy and artistry are meaningful values in the teaching profession. But they are counterproductive, even obtuse ones, in instances where teachers or administrators are trying to learn complex new skills that others have mastered and for which experts have worked out ways to help novices progress rapidly and with a minimum of wreckage.

The second parable completes the picture. Imagine that you try to cross a large, unfamiliar city at rush hour. Let's make it worse: a large, unfamiliar, *foreign* city. You take out your map, find the main axis, look for the signs for the next destination, and creep erratically along, behind a seemingly endless stream of trucks and fellow cars, many with foreign licence plates like yours. With any luck, you are across the city in an hour.

Now assume you are crossing your *own* city at rush hour. You take one look at the main axis and turn off into a warren of smaller streets, many of them one-way and many of them without traffic lights. If you hit a long line of traffic, you change directions, weaving your way laterally for a while, then picking up a street that parallels the main axis route out of the city. You may even go *away* from your destination for a few moments, because you know that at 5 p.m., on a secondary road you usually take, there is construction underway, but not on another chain of roads slightly to the east. If all goes well, you have been moving virtually the whole time and you are across the city in twenty minutes.

The early stages of implementation look like the traverse of the foreign city and the later stages like the traverse of the familiar one. For your own city, you have a detailed cognitive *map*, an articulated representation of the streets and the traffic patterns. And you have a repository of experience telling you what to do when, at 5 p.m., there are fifteen cars in front of you at a given traffic light. You have elaborated that map very gradually, literally by driving each one of those patterns hundreds of times, then inferring the most promising combinations that correspond to different moments of the day. In other words, you need the cognitive map to make ever more appropriate choices and you got the cognitive map by trying out multiple combinations of each choice.

Both the elaboration of the map and the trails take time. And both profit from expert advice. Also, both call for different configurations of assistance. If someone showed you a film of the city you have just come to live in, then outlined on a chart the three quickest ways to get across it at rush hour – this is what much pre-service training for innovation implementation looks like – you would forget this information almost immediately. Five months later, however, the same film and the same chart might be invaluable – because you are now ready to take them in. What we have learned in the study of implementation is how to provide different forms of support at different stages of the process of learning – or relearning – one's own city, instructionally speaking.

A few reminders

For virtually all of the points made earlier, Michael Fullan's text, along with the *New Meaning of Change*, are valuable primers. But I want to close with a few issues which may be instructive to frame somewhat differently.

The first is this: implementation is a political process, one that involves conflict. What constitutes school 'improvement' for some means 'rubbish' for others, at least initially. What planners of educational change may construe as 'support', some users construe as intrusiveness or belittling. Or again: if the innovation in question reduces my teaching hours in Latin – as many tend to do – I would be a fool to play along, unless there was an alternative I could live with. Similarly, many changes are introduced as the result of external political pressures and, like increases in the price of oil, these pressures are then passed along down the chain: to the senior school administration, then to the district administrators, then to the principals, then to the teachers, then to the pupils and their parents. In all cases, unless there is a real crisis or an undreamed-of consensus, this process entails some people spending more time and energy than they would have spontaneously chosen to – even doing something they don't consider worthwhile. To get them to do this, something more than a 'shared vision' and a social technology of implementation are often required. The same dynamics are in effect when the pressures go in the opposite direction: from needs or urgencies expressed at the classroom level, then demanded of principals who then send the message upward that solutions cannot be put off, much as senior officials might prefer doing just that.

What typically happens is that there are usually dozens of bargains being struck along the way. Try out this programme and we'll get some interesting materials and training. Let the principal have her visibility from this new project and she'll let us modify it to suit our purposes or our constraints. Tell the inspector that we'll go ahead if he agrees to suspend the standardized tests in the experimental classes for two years. Tell the teachers that we'll set set up a facility for immigrant children if they'll accept to raise the class size so we can release staff for this new project.

These bargains, moreover, are usually *implicit* ones. All sides know one another well enough to get the right signals, and know that making such agreements explicit is asking for trouble when they fall into the wrong hands. And *because* these negotiations are handled implicitly, we might make the mistake of assuming that implementation is a straightforward affair of setting things right, introducing promising new practices, meeting new or old objectives more efficiently. In fact, it is no more straightforward than in other micro-political arenas of social life. Simply, we in the educational business have something like a moral mandate to under-emphasize, at least in public, the more distasteful aspects of social behaviour. So when we talk about educational change, or even when we execute it, we may paper over the more irrational, conflictual, subtly authoritarian aspects of its execution. We are often guilty of rhetorical angelism. This, in turn, leaves us vulnerable to visions of educational change that are coated variously in language that is altruistic, semi-religious, military or derived from mechanical engineering. If we actually conducted the process as if it were a purely technical or spiritual affair, we would be in serious trouble very quickly. At the same time, we would be wrong to veer to the other extreme, conducting implementation in a field of power relationships and as a sequence of negotiations giving rise to periodic 'agreements'. By doing that, we would be throwing away the intrinsic altruism and idealism that permeates the educational enterprise and that mobilize people to take on moments of uncertainty in the name of something larger than their individual interests.

A second warning. To read *Successful School Improvement* may be, in fact, a depressing experience for many school administrators. Have a look, for example, at the several lists of support mechanisms associated with successful implementation or those describing 'purposeful leadership' of effective schools (strengthening the school improvement culture, shared power and responsibility, effective communication, wise mix of resources, use of multiple leverage points, protecting users from undue demands, etc.). As a school principal perusing this list, I may conclude that Michael Fullan is talking about supermen and superwomen in privileged settings or, if not, that I am inadequate in my job.

I think there are three, interrelated problems here. First, we are dealing with studies of exceptional cases. One kind of study design calls for our contrasting successful attempts at implementing change with unsuccessful ones, then isolating the characteristics of administrators (or teachers, or consultants) that distinguish the two sets. Another consists of case studies of highly successful projects or institutions, from which we extract the influence of administrators. What the 'exceptional' principals do and the others do not then becomes a key explanation for the relative success of the change enacted.

The problem is that, by working with extreme cases, we are not represent-ing the majority of schools. We are also assuming some kind of linear scale from the 'poor' principals to the 'exceptional' ones, whereas this may not be the case in real life. The middle of the scale, where most of the cases are, may look very different. Also, on consulting this list of executive or managerial 'strengths', we may get the impression that all or most of the principals dis-played them. In fact, the characteristics are usually derived from dozens of distinct cases, then compiled into a 'grand list'. At any one, real-life site, the principal may have exemplified only one or two of the facets on the master list. We may never find an actual site with all the requisite characteristics of leader-ship and management.

This brings me directly to the second point. There are exceptional and appalling schools and school administrators, to be sure. But most are garden-variety ones – with weaknesses and strengths, with a few virtuosi and many more humdrum staff, along with some fairly problematic people. *This* has to be the starting-point for talking about the introduction of educational change. At most sites, we will not have the corps of exceptional administrators or consul-tants described in this text. Nor will we necessarily be able to train them to these levels or to recruit them from elsewhere, if they are already trained. We will have to assume that we are a relatively flawed little enterprise – like most – trying to correct a few of those flaws with the means at our disposal. In other words, it would be an error to assume that an average school district or school can replicate many of the conditions described in this text that contribute to, or even produce, significant changes in local practices. In that respect, in fact, many of the research data in this book are probably best read as inspirational rather than as prescriptive for any given case.

Finally, Michael Fullan banks heavily in this text on the determining influ-ence of people at other points than at the locus of actual implementation – in the classroom, or in the project centre or in the remedial laboratory. To a great extent – I may be overstating this – he believes that superintendents, principals and consultants can actually 'bring about' behavioural and attitudinal changes in other people who will be executing them. Implementation in this view seems to ride heavily on enlightened mixtures of charisma, knowledgeability, power, competence, consideration of users' needs. To be sure, there is much research to support that view. Much of it, however, has trained its light exclusively on these very administrators and consultants, and on the ways in which other actors, teachers for example, perceive them. By doing so, it automatically magnifies their influence.

It may be that, if we come down a notch, the world would look differently. What is the pupil's eye view of the change process, month to month? What are the experiences of users, *independently* of what supervisory people do or don't do? After all, in the course of a given innovation, users have relatively little contact, in terms of hours spent together, with their supervisors. (For that matter, most teachers have very little contact with major innovations in the course of their 40-year careers; they are exceptional events). Maybe we have overestimated the power and influence of people above or outside the core activities carried out by others – no matter how exceptional these people may be? Maybe we have *under*estimated the influence of these street-level imple-menters actually to determine how much change is enacted, and to do it in ways that no outsider can really assess without being at the loci of implementa-tion for extended periods of time? These are nasty questions, but they may not be inappropriate ones.

A last reflection I would leave readers with: can we assume that the school building is always the proper locus of school improvement? For Michael Full-an, continuous improvement at the building level is a central issue, and so he concentrates many of his efforts there.

It is worth asking for example, if, in a large secondary school, we can talk about the 'building'. Or rather, do we often have a set of loosely connected, balkanized departments, each with its own norms and conventions? And it is a long, tenuous reach from the principal's office, through department heads, to the troops. At each juncture, wondrous transformations may occur. In their recent research, for instance, Milbrey McLaughlin, Judith Little and Joan Tal-bert found it difficult to identify a school 'culture' as much more than an agglomeration of the several sub-cultures in secondary schools (McLaughlin *et al.* 1990). There was often greater variation within schools than between them.

Similarly, in smaller places, how much transformation can we reasonably hope for? Oftentimes, smaller schools are places where people have come to form cliques, durable affections, durable hatreds. In many primary schools, where there is no forum for self-analysis, or even for clearing up misunder-standings, interpersonal relationships can fester. During moments of change, remarks on the conduct of the project can quickly be construed as personal slights. That smaller schools are often emotional hothouses tells us that the interpersonal dimensions of managing change may in fact be the most import-ant ones.

There are some experiments underway which suggest that *sets* of schools, organized into task forces, may be promising ways of enacting 'clusters' of change in each contributing unit. The collective stimulation, the possibility of 'de-centring' from one's own surround, the novelty of the situation and some of the actors, the greater wealth of ideas and instructional expertise are all additional resources. Biology teachers in curriculum reforms may go further with one another across schools, even on questions of evaluation or group interactions, than interdisciplinary groups from a single school. Fellow third and fourth grade teachers from several schools may have more to tell and teach one another – and may do it more easily – than full-school teams implementing independently the same innovation. In fact, when we move from 'implemen-tation' to 'continuous improvement', a cross-institutional model, organized into teams and networks each working on circumscribed projects, may in some cases be a better design than an intra-institutional reform. The role of the principal, then, becomes more one of articulating these sub-projects with the objectives and operations within her institution than of leading and managing the process from the top.

These are not exclusive scenarios. They do, however, widen the range of what is possible. In so doing, they better the chances that a given school or school district will be able to find a design that is appropriate to its purposes, to its peculiar context, to the distinctive innovation under consideration, and to one particular point in time. To do that, however – to choose and combine wisely – requires a good understanding of the process as a whole and of its component parts. Clearly, the accumulated experience, research and wisdom of the implementation literature is a fount for managing the process successfully.

References

Fullan, M. (1982) *The Meaning of Educational Change.* New York, Teachers' College Press; Toronto, OISE Press.

Fullan, M. with Stiegelbauer, S. (1991) *The New Meaning of Educational Change.* London, Cassells; New York, Teachers' College Press; Toronto, OISE Press.

Fullan, M. and Pomfret, A. (1977) Research on curriculum and instruction implementation. *Review of Educational Research*, 5(47), 335–97.

Hall, G.E. and Loucks, S. (1977) A developmental model for determining whether the treatment is actually implemented. *American Educational Research Journal*, 14(3), 263–76.

Huberman, M. and Miles, M. (1984) *Innovation Up Close.* New York, Plenum.

Joyce, B. and Showers, B. (1988) *Student Achievement through Staff Development.* New York, Longman.

McLaughlin, M., Talbert, J. and Bascia, N. (eds) (1990) *The Contexts of Teaching in the Secondary School.* New York, Teachers' College Press.

Yin, R.K. and White, J.L. (1984) *Microcomputer Implementation in Schools.* Washington, DC, COSMOS Corporation.

1 Successful School Improvement and the Implementation Perspective

Remarkably, the history of the careful study of the educational change process is quite young. It is only since the 1960s that we have been able to understand how educational change works in practice. We have come to call the decade of the 1960s the *adoption* era, because educators were preoccupied with how many innovations of the day were being 'taken on', or adopted. It was a period of new maths, new chemistry and physics, open education, individualized instruction, team teaching, and so on. Innovations, the more the better, became the mark of progress.

Around 1970, almost overnight, innovation got a bad name. The term 'implementation' – what was happening (or not happening) in practice – came into use. Goodlad and his colleagues' *Behind the Classroom Door* (1970), Sarason's *The Culture of the School and the Problem of Change* (1971), Gross and associates' *Implementing Organizational Innovations* (1971), and Smith and Keith's *Anatomy of Educational Innovation* (1971), all published at the turn of the decade, exposed the problem. Innovations were being adopted without anyone asking why (change for the sake of change), and no forethought was being given to follow-through. Charter and Jones (1973) captured it succinctly in referring to the problem of evaluating innovations as 'the risk of appraising non-events'.

Implementation focuses on what happens in practice. It is concerned with the nature and extent of actual change, as well as the factors and processes that influence how and what changes are achieved. More broadly, *the implementation perspective* captures both the content and process of contending with new ideas, programmes, activities, structures, policies, etc. new to the people involved. In particular, the implementation perspective concerns itself with whether any change has *actually* occurred in practice. It demonstrates a bias for action in attempting to understand and influence improvements at the level of practice.

There are two main reasons why it is important to focus on implementation. The first is that we do not know what has changed (if anything) unless we attempt to conceptualize and measure it directly. We cannot view policies or innovations as simply entering or being generated by the system and somehow

producing outcomes. Without knowing what's in the 'black box' of implementation, we do not know how to interpret the outcomes (or absence of
outcomes). Is failure due to implementing poor ideas, or to the inability to
implement good ideas? Is success due to a well–implemented innovation, or to
some extraneous factor? In short, without implementation data we cannot link
particular changes to learning outcomes.

A second reason why it is important to examine implementation is to
understand some of the reasons why so many educational innovations and
reforms fail. By investigating implementation directly we can begin to identify
the reasons why innovations fail or succeed.

Finally, by way of introduction, I would caution the reader about the term
implementation. It can have the connotation of a 'thing to be implemented'
thereby having an external-in or top-down bias. Knowledge of the implementation process can be used to attempt to impose one's favourite solution. This
would be a misuse and a misunderstanding of the findings from implementation research. Values and meaning are central to implementation success (Fullan 1991). The implementation perspective can be valuable only if one
understands the total set of findings *in combination*. The process of change,
which enables all participants to sort out the pros and cons of different innovations and directions, will be the successful process. The implementation
perspective, if understood deeply and authentically, can be a powerful resource
for accomplishing *real* improvements in classrooms and schools.

Innovation, teacher development and school development

It is essential to understand the relationship of implementation not only to
innovation and teacher development but also to school development. Stated
simply, implementation is learning to do and learning to understand something
new. Change in other words is a process of learning new ideas and things.

The link of implementation to innovation is rather straightforward (although frequently neglected). An innovation – a new or revised curriculum, a
policy, a structure, an idea – is something that is new to the people encounter-
ing it for the first time. Dealing with an innovation effectively means alterations in *behaviours* and *beliefs*. Changes in behaviours – new skills, activities,
practices – and changes in beliefs – new understandings, commitments – are at
the core of implementation. Thus the key issue from an implementation
perspective is how the process of change unfolds *vis-à-vis* what people *do*
(behaviours) and *think* (beliefs) in relation to a particular innovation.

Many innovations are introduced in a manner that does not involve doing
and thinking, and as such they have a superficial or negative effect. Stating it
this way does not assume that all innovations are good and should be implemented. Failure to implement an ill–conceived or a poorly developed policy, or
a bad idea is obviously a good thing. But assuming that we are attempting to
sort out and implement promising new ideas, the implementation perspective
forces us to confront what is actually happening in practice. It makes us, if you

like, pay more attention to getting results. Focusing on assessing change in practice even forces us to reject certain innovations for good reason (as distinct from superficial or extraneous reasons) if we find them wanting.

Considerable research has been conducted on identifying factors related to successful implementation and on unravelling the process of change as these factors interact. Chapter 2 provides a good case illustration of this research through an examination of new policies and practices on microcomputers.

Teacher development is another core concept for implementation. I find it helpful to consider it both specifically for given particular innovations, and generically in relation to how teachers develop over time or over their careers. Again the specific connection to innovation and implementation is explicit. If implementation involves new behaviours and beliefs, teacher development in relation to these new learnings is a *sine qua non*. This is why in-service and professional development in support of specific innovations is usually found to be the critical factor for success (see Huberman and Miles 1984).

A long-term view of teacher development is more complex. One could stay with the innovation theme and say that long-term teacher development involves the ever-increasing expansion of the teachers' repertoire by success-fully implementing one innovation after another. In other words, teachers would more or less continuously innovate – adding, subtracting, integrating and refining their practices and reflections. But given the way that innovations come and go, this would likely amount to a piece-meal, fragmented set of experiences.

Alternatively, instead of moving from innovation to teacher development one could reverse the direction, and examine what teacher development looks like as one views the changing sea of innovations. I take such a teacher de-velopment perspective in Chapter 6 (see also Fullan *et al.* 1990a; Fullan 1991). Ultimately, what is important is the capacity of teachers – individually and with others – to manage change continuously. This means the ability to find mean-ing among an array of innovative possibilities, and to become adept at knowing when to seek change aggressively, and when to back off. To do this teachers must understand the implementation perspective and the change process, or they will be at the mercy of external forces of change. Elsewhere, Andy Hargreaves and I have provided a set of guidelines for teachers designed to give them more control over the change process (Fullan and Hargreaves 1991).

School development, another key construct, is deeply relevant to both spe-cific innovations, and to generic teacher and school development. Relative to the former, specific innovations are more readily implemented in certain kinds of school climates. This relationship is tied directly to what we know about the implementation process. Since implementation involves learning to do some-thing new, it follows that schools that foster a learning orientation among their staff as well as their students are more likely to bring about improvements. If there is strong collegiality coupled with a commitment to continuous improve-ment, backed up by policies and structures designed to support purposeful teacher interaction, the chances of working through an implementation pro-cess are much greater. Some schools are more isolationist or 'stuck', while others are more collaborative or 'moving' (Rosenholtz 1989). The effective schools research, of course, has demonstrated rather conclusively the relationship between these types of characteristics and effective change (e.g. Mortimore *et al.* 1988). There are very few lone innovators. Implementation occurs when teachers interact with and support each other as they try out new practices, cope with difficulties, develop new skills and so on. We know that early implementation is fraught with difficulties, and the school more than any other level can provide the kind of environment necessary to address inevitable implementation problems.

As we shift from considering the school as the *context* for innovation, to the school as the *target* of change we move to more basic or generic questions of school development. The question is no longer, what are the characteristics of more effective schools, but rather how can schools become more effective. How can schools *qua* schools move from individualistic to collaborative work cultures with all that that entails. Chapter 5 in particular analyses this issue of school or institutional development. It is generic in the sense that when schools become collaborative they have a greater capacity to manage all change, not just *x* or *y* innovation. This is definitely not to say that they implement all changes they encounter, but that they have a greater critical capacity to cope, even resist inappropriate innovations, while being able to forge the combination of changes that works to achieve desired goals (Fullan 1991).

Thus teacher development and school development are very intimately related. As one goes so does the other. The implementation perspective has enabled us first to understand this relationship in terms of how individual innovations fare, and inevitably has led us to the deeper issues of how teacher development and school development *per se* must be the focus of long-term change strategies.

These discoveries have also helped to clarify the various roles. The principal or head, for example, needs both to be concerned about particular innovations at hand, as well as attending to mid- to longer-term teacher and school development. Chapter 4 delves into this pivotal role. Since the school is the centre of change, the head of the school plays a critical role for better or for worse.

Similarly, the districts' or local authorities' role becomes clearer. They are to provide the combination of pressure and support needed to influence and co-ordinate teacher development and school development over time. Individual schools can become innovative despite the district's role, but they cannot *stay* innovative despite the district. Chapter 3 uses a case study to examine how one district evolved to become more effective at co-ordinating and influencing the capacity of the system to manage change.

Perspectives on the change process

The implementation process is complex and dilemma ridden, but we have accumulated considerable knowledge and insight into the process of change during the 1980s. Some of these lessons were not self-evident at the outset, although they make common sense once discovered. The main revelations in this journey include a combination of elements that we usually think of as mutually exclusive or as not operating in the manner that they do. There are four main insights that were not predictable, but have turned out to be important:

1 active initiation and participation
2 pressure and support
3 changes in behaviour and beliefs
4 the overriding problem of ownership.

The first issue is how can reform get started when there are large numbers of people involved. There is no single answer, but it is increasingly clear that changes require some impetus to get started. There is no evidence that widespread involvement at the initiation stage is either feasible or effective. It is more likely the case that small groups of people begin and, if successful, build momentum. Active initiation, starting small and thinking big, bias for action, and learning by doing are all aspects of making change more manageable, by getting the process underway in a desirable direction. Participation, initiative-taking and empowerment are key factors from the beginning, but sometimes do not get activated until a change process has begun.

Second, it is increasingly clear that both pressure and support are necessary for success. We usually think of pressure as a bad thing, and support as good. But there is a positive role for pressure in change. There are many forces maintaining the status quo. When change occurs it is because some pressure has built up that leads to action. During the change process interaction among implementers serves to integrate both pressure and support. One of the reasons that peer coaching works so effectively is that it combines pressure and support in a kind of seamless way. Successful change projects always include elements of both pressure and support. Pressure without support leads to resistance and alienation; support without pressure leads to drift or waste of resources.

Third, the relationship between changes in behaviour and changes in beliefs or understanding requires careful consideration. Returning to the theme of meaning, it seems that most people do not discover new understandings until they have delved into something. In many cases, changes in behaviour precede rather than follow changes in belief (Fullan 1985). Moreover, when people try something new they often suffer what I call 'the implementation dip'. Things get worse before they get better as people grapple with the meaning and skills of change (Joyce and Showers 1988). We see then that the relationship between behavioural and belief change is reciprocal and ongoing, with change in doing or behaviour a necessary experience on the way to breakthroughs in meaning and understanding.

The role of ownership is the fourth subtlety in the change process. Clearly, deep ownership of something new on the part of large numbers of people is tantamount to real change, but the fact is that ownership is not acquired that easily. And when people are apparently in favour of a particular change, they may not 'own it' in the sense of understanding it and being skilled at it, that is they may not know what they are doing. Ownership in the sense of clarity, skill and commitment is a progressive process. True ownership is not something that occurs magically at the beginning, but rather is something that comes out the other end of a successful change process. In successful change projects ownership is stronger in the middle of the process than it was at the beginning, and stronger still at the end. In effect, successful improvement can be best thought of as a process of *mobilization* and *positive contagion*.

In summary, the broad implications of the implementation process have several interrelated components. The first is that the crux of change involves the development of meaning in relation to a new idea, programme, reform or set of activities. But it is *individuals* who have to develop new meaning, and these individuals are insignificant parts of a gigantic, loosely organized, complex, messy social system that contains myriad different subjective worlds.

The causes of change also became more easily identifiable and understood once we possess an underlying conception of what constitutes change as a process over time. The factors of implementation and continuation reinforce or undercut each other as an interrelated system. Single-factor theories of change are doomed to failure. Arguments that product quality is more important than teacher attitude, or that external factors are more important than internal ones, or that teachers are more central than administrators, are pointless. Effective implementation depends on the *combination* of factors and themes discussed in this book. The characteristics of the nature of the change, the make-up of the local district, the character of individual schools and teachers, and the existence and form of external relationships interact to produce conditions for change or non-change. It takes a fortunate combination of the right factors – a critical mass – to support and guide the process of re-learning, which respects the maintenance needs of individuals and groups and at the same time facilitates, stimulates and prods people to change through a process of incremental and decremental fits and starts on the way to institutionalizing (or, if appropriate, rejecting) the change in question.

We understand that not all change is progress, or even meant to be. As individuals react incorrectly to pressures, so do school districts and societies. There are many motivations and origins for educational change, and in retrospect only a fraction of them seem to be based on the identification of a clear and important educational need and on the development of a quality idea and programme. Even if we get the need and the idea right, the sheer complexity of the process of implementation has, as it were, a sociological mind of its own, which frequently defies management even when all parties have the best of intentions. After twenty-five years of ripping off and ripping into the system, we have learned 'the pathos of implementation': faithful implementation is sometimes undesirable (because the idea is bad), sometimes impossible (because power won't permit), and often unforeseeable (because it depends on what people bring to it as well as what's in it) (Majone and Wildavsky 1978: 25).

The odds against successful school improvement are not small. Increasing our understanding of implementation may alter them. The theory of the meaning of change and the change process provides us with an underlying conception of what should be done. This guide to change enables us to locate specific factors, to observe how they work in concrete situations and to explain why they function as they do, and with what consequences for school improvement.

In other words, successful school improvement – pursued throughout this book – depends on an understanding of the problem of change at the level of practice and the development of corresponding strategies for bringing about beneficial reforms.

2 The Implementation of Microcomputers in Schools: A Case Study*

The implementation perspective is valuable for examining specific innovations and policies. One of the more central innovations in the past few years has been microcomputers in the classroom. It is both a policy phenomenon (in the sense that school districts and states/provinces advocate/require the use of new technologies) and an innovation problem (in the sense that various groups are genuinely attempting to implement more effective uses of microcomputers).

In this chapter, I take as a case study the large-scale attempt in Ontario, Canada to implement the widespread use of microcomputers in classrooms and schools. This case is particularly illustrative of the implementation perspective as it applies to the factors and processes involved in putting into practice a major new policy.

Implementing microcomputers in schools contains all that is fascinating in educational change: intuitive attraction and great uncertainty; excitement and hardship; enthusiasm and exhaustion; visibility and high public interest combined with unknown results. Ontario's expectations and approach to implementing new educational technologies (NET) in schools ups the stakes involved.† Sponsoring the development of its own microcomputer, funding the development of software geared to official curriculum goals and policy, focusing on the integration of computers into the total learning experiences of students: Ontario's approach is comprehensive. The technical accomplishments are considerable, but the knowledge and skill demands on teachers are huge. NET in Ontario is an ambitious innovation. The task is sizeable and multifaceted. While there is strong 'front-end' financial support in launching NET, there is at this point a great need to build a knowledge-based strategy focusing on the 'up-close' realities of using microcomputers in everyday classrooms.

The current focus of implementation in Ontario is to assist teachers in

---

* This chapter has been adapted from Fullan *et al.* (1988).
† We use the terms microcomputers and NET interchangeably.

learning to use microcomputers and approved educational software with students. The Ministry of Education permits the use of any microcomputers, but it has also heavily subsidized the development of a commercial microcomputer called ICON. The ministry has specified the requirements for grant eligible microcomputer systems (GEMS) based on the ICON, and provides grants to school boards to purchase eligible machines. In addition, the ministry has funded the development of new software which is based on official ministry curriculum guidelines; such software is disseminated under contract by the Ontario Educational Software Service (OESS), which is operated by the provincial educational television authority, TVOntario.

I use the implementation perspective in this chapter to analyse the key implementation processes and factors associated with the attempting to put into practice more effective uses of microcomputers in classrooms in Ontario. I refer to the general problem as implementing New Educational Technologies (NET). The basic question is: how does our implementation knowledge help us to understand the phenomenon of implementing microcomputers.

The most useful place to start is with an overview of the implementation change process (Figure 2.1).

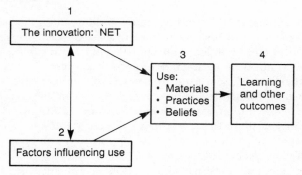

Figure 2.1 An overview of implementation

To start with Box 3, we can ask the direct question, 'What types of things would have changed in the classroom if NET were to be implemented?' While it is an oversimplification, we could say that these images cover at least three aspects or dimensions of change for the teacher in the classroom:

1 the use of *new hardware and software* materials
2 the use of *new activities* (including grouping) behaviours or practices
3 changes in *beliefs and understanding*.

The use of new materials (hardware and software) is the most obvious because it is concrete and tangible. One can observe materials, and can readily answer the question of whether microcomputers are actually being used in the classroom. The second and third dimensions are much more fundamental and problematic because they involve, respectively, changes in what teachers do (practices and underlying skills) and think (beliefs and understandings).

Table 2.1   Factors influencing implementation

Characteristics of the innovation/NET

 1 Clarity and complexity
 2 Consensus and conflict about the change
 3 Quality and practicality of the change

Local conditions

 4 Central office direction, commitment and support
 5 Process for implementation and institutionalization
 6 Professional development and assistance
 7 Implementation monitoring and problem–solving
 8 Principal's leadership
 9 Community support
10 Environmental stability

Especially in the use of NET we maintain that the pedagogical use of software – the most effective teaching practices in relation to particular pieces of software – and the corresponding conceptual understanding *vis à vis* particular software are (1) not well specified, developed or known; (2) are complex; and (3) are at the heart of successful or unsuccessful implementation. We also suggest that the production of software *per se*, will *not* resolve this problem (although it is one important step in that direction). Pedagogical uses of new technology that relate to the use of new skills and to new understandings are what will count. Without such new learning, the supported learning outcome (Box 4) will not be achieved.

The next question is, 'What factors (Box 2) influence the likelihood of effective use?' I focus on ten factors known to influence implementation use (see Table 2.1). In each case I contrast the ministry's perspective (labelled the *Broad Picture*) with implementation data from the school and school board level (labelled *Up Close*).

In considering these factors it is useful to keep three additional components of our implementation perspective in mind. First, implementation is a developmental process of change for teachers attempting to use an innovation, which can involve alterations in materials, instructional practices and beliefs about the teacher/learning process. Second, implementation is the second phase in a three-phase process of innovation – initiation (mobilization, adoption), implementation and institutionalization (continuation, incorporation). Third, the factors operate as a system of variables over time. They are mutually reinforcing, and the strategic importance and activities associated with any one factor can vary at different phases in the overall process.

The evidence is very strong that the ten factors and associated processes directly affect the quality of use of large-scale innovations. We draw on interviews and secondary research studies to discuss the broad picture as it is perceived by policy-makers and the local or up-close picture as seen by individual implementors. The implementation perspective above all is subjective. The *meaning* as experienced by individual implementors is what counts (Fullan 1991).

Characteristics of the innovation/NET

Clarity and complexity

In order for implementation to succeed, implementors have to gain a clear understanding of what to do and change in order to put the innovation into practice. Policies, written guides, in-service programmes, and participation in innovation development can help clarify the meaning of change for those involved. True understanding, however, comes only when teachers are given opportunities and time to work with the innovation in the classroom and to talk about what they are doing with others.

Some educational innovations are more complex to implement than others. For individual implementors, innovation complexity arises from the number of components of practice affected, the degree of difference from existing practices, materials and beliefs, and the difficulty of learning to make the necessary changes. While more complex innovations requiring major changes are harder to gain clarity about and more difficult to implement, they are also more likely to yield non-trivial results than innovations which demand less personal effort and organizational support.

One of the dangers of complex innovations is that implementors may develop a sense of false clarity if they only incorporate the easy to learn features of the innovation into their practice. Or if the change is experienced to be complex and overwhelming without substantial progress, users often give up 'down-size' or trivialize the change (see Huberman and Miles 1984). In either case, the expected impact of the innovation will likewise be reduced.

Clarity: broad picture

Ministry officials emphasize that there is still great uncertainty about student outcomes and about effective organization and use of the technologies in schools, particularly in their use to support creative learning. They see a need to foster variation in use initially and to identify effective use through research. The macro-level picture is less one of teachers coming to understand the use of proven practices during implementation, than of teacher understanding during early implementation resulting in increasingly precise and convergent knowledge about the characteristics of effective technologies and their use.

Ministry attention to the needs of school system personnel for clarity about the implementation of province-approved materials has focused mainly on giving policy direction through policy/programme memorandums and statements about computer applications in new or revised curriculum guidelines, and on controlling the characteristics of hardware and software. Two key objectives of the ministry's hardware and software development strategies are to standardize the equipment and materials in the schools and to make the technologies as easy-to-use as possible for teachers and students. Software developers contracted by the ministry must specify in their programme design such things as users, objectives, software type, roles, tracking strategies and suggestions for incorporating the software into the curriculum and classroom.

Clarity: up close
Findings from school-level studies of early users indicate that getting clear understanding of what to do and change is difficult for teachers, despite provincial pronouncements and the best efforts of software developers.

Field test reports on approved materials highlight the difficulty teachers have understanding how programmes work and could be used, and what role teachers should play.

> The actual instruction role of the lessonware in some field-tests might have been different from the intended role because of a failure to distinguish between material intended for initial presentation and material for review or practice.
>
> (Pike 1985)

> A principal difficulty with the SHAPEMATE program is that students and teachers alike do not understand how to operate the program. In almost all cases, they needed to be carefully shown how to use the program and what could be achieved with it. Also, they fail to appreciate its full capability.
>
> (Gillis 1985)

> Many programs fail to explain the teacher's role. As a result teachers frequently underestimate the amount of guidance certain programs require, particularly simulations. This is a common factor in many otherwise sound programs that fail to live up to expectations and draw teacher criticism.
>
> (Gillis 1986)

Such findings cast doubt on the notion that increased specificity in software documentation is likely to produce the degree of implementor clarity needed for effective utilization. We maintain and shall elaborate later that attention needs to be shifted to identifying and developing effective *teaching practices* in relation to each software program.

These examples suggest that even a combination of state-of-the-art software, explicit directions and intensive initial in-service may not be powerful enough to produce clear and full understanding of the innovation during the *early* period of change.

Complexity: broad picture
The first order of complexity for the Ministry of Education is simply dealing with the organizational magnitude of the installed base goals, that is placing

microcomputers in the classrooms of 100,000 teachers and developing and distributing educational software covering all grade levels and areas of the curriculum. These necessary mobilization-oriented concerns have tended to overshadow the complexity of using the technologies, once they are in place.

While not much supportive action has been taken as yet, officials interviewed do convey an awareness of several aspects of the complexity of NET implementation for users. Their description of ideal utilization demonstrates a sense that 'full implementation' of the technologies would affect and alter many components of teaching practice (e.g. teacher and student roles and relationships, teaching and learning activities, classroom organization, content, pacing, evaluation and record-keeping) and could involve fundamental changes in teacher beliefs about the nature of learning and the role of the teacher.

The ministry envisions the new technologies being used to support such long-standing educational aims as the following: accommodation of a variety of student learning styles and needs, individualization of student programmes, development of critical thinking skills and skills in the process of learning, developing skills in decision-making and in collaborating with others, and fostering positive attitudes towards self and learning. Although ministry expectations regarding use of the technologies are consistent with existing policy images of the learner and learning process, ministry officials believe the degree of change confronting teachers differs from that associated with routine curriculum changes.

> We'd like to encourage recognition that teachers are starting from base zero. It's not like a new content guideline. They are not implementing a rehash of what they already know. We need to recognize the fact that it is a major growth for teachers.

They talk about potential major changes in classroom organization (physical arrangements, timetables, grouping and teacher roles), and the long-term process that will be required to develop the full potential of new technologies.

Complexity: up close

Data on teacher-level NET implementation highlights the complexity problem as experienced by teachers. Field data indicate that microcomputer implementation is often a difficult experience even for interested teachers using high-quality software with good organizational supports.

The frustration and difficulty of beginning implementation is a common theme. Similarities are evident in examples of beginning implementation from Carmichael *et al.*'s (1985) study of the unsupported (i.e. no training or consultative assistance) use of Logo, and from Lee's (1986) studies of microcomputer use during and following an intensive inservice course on the use of approved microcomputers.

Unsupported initial implementation

[Classroom setting/teacher report] some pupils are overbearing. Constant interruptions. Teaching today was a bust. I felt like I lived in the centre of a three-ring circus. I solved this problem by giving a structured lesson.

[Computer lab/teacher report] . . . the first trip to the computer room was overwhelming . . . I found that I could spend no time with any one group. I will not go there again until there are more disks and some help. I have found this experience of no benefit to the children and too over-whelming for me.

(Carmichael *et al.* 1985)

Supported initial implementation

One Grade 8 teacher noted at the end of the 16-hour inservice course that she was still uncomfortable, worried and nervous about teaching the EDIT and LOGO programs to her students. She felt helpless and frus-trated when computer problems arose and things went wrong which she did not know how to fix.

(Lee 1986)

[Another teacher] was a reluctant and a near non-user during the inser-vice training period last year. He claimed to have no computer back-ground whatsoever, and did not understand why the computer acted strangely when he pressed the keys. He found the 16-hour inservice training very confusing and frustrating because it covered too many things in too short a time. He felt that he could not, and did not, absorb all that new learning at once. To him, this first computer experience was a total disaster and most unrewarding. He avoided the computer like the plague.

(Lee 1986)

While we cannot say with certainty how typical these examples were for all teachers involved in NET use in these two situations, such findings recall those reported for other educational innovations involving substantial change in practice, in that beginning implementation is characterized by frustration and difficulty organizing and managing use of the innovation. They also echo the findings in Huberman and Miles (1984) in depth case studies of educational innovations that early implementation of major changes is frustrating and diffi-cult, no matter how much initial assistance is provided.

Consensus and conflict about the change

The prospects for successful implementation are greater when those expected to carry out a change agree on the need, on the appropriateness of the innova-tions selected, and on the priority of the change effort relative to other local concerns. While educational innovations are often adopted without wide-spread initial agreement on the need for change and choice of solutions, this does not necessarily spell failure. Teacher acceptance and commitment can develop during implementation when other conditions are favourable (e.g. effective innovations, administrative commitment, adequate assistance). Of course, the consensus of administrators and other stakeholders, such as trustees and parents, is also important.

Consensus and conflict: broad picture

Ministry officials recognize that the general movement towards microcomputer use in education reflects grass-roots interest and initiative. They see widespread parent support for implementation and a core group of teacher supporters. According to their current 'guesstimates' (derived from such sources as teacher training statistics), about 20 per cent of the elementary and secondary teacher population are probably enthusiastic or moderately committed computer users. The other 80 per cent are basically 'uncommitted' at the present time. In the words of one official, 'we still face a tremendous problem with teacher attitudes about use of the technology'.

The official policy places the priority on exploiting the creative learning potential of the technologies (rather than limiting use to remediation, drill and content delivery), and hardware and software initiatives support that direction. Ministry policy also favours integration of computer-based learning materials and activities into all subject areas of the curriculum, rather than treating computers and computer applications as a separate course of studies (except in secondary Computer Studies courses).

There is not a clear sense at the level of the ministry of the degree to which teachers and students using microcomputers and software agree with those priorities. There is a fear that implementation could be stymied by entrenched views about the structure of the curriculum and opposition to change.

> There are strong mind sets hindering change in the curricula. Over the years, there have been expansions in curriculum content and in clientele, such as special education, but we're used to the traditional curriculum model. Use of microcomputer technologies suggests a new model. Software integrates the curriculum. It can work against a subject approach.

A final aspect of consensus concerns the relative local priority accorded to NET implementation. Ministry officials are highly sensitive to the fact that continued financial support from the government is critical to accomplishment of its NET implementation goals. The basic approach to maintaining local priority is through special funding, requiring board implementation plans, doing all possible to make the tools workable and worth the teachers' effort, and tying NET applications into all new provincial curriculum projects.

Consensus and conflict: up close

Grass-roots support of the need for microcomputers and educational software in the schools is well-documented. Evidence of widespread local parent support is reported in the studies of Larter and Fitzgerald (1983) and Carmichael *et al.* (1985), and is described more fully in the up-close analysis of Community Support. However, an important message from the field is that mere availability and access to the technologies is not sufficient to create 'their need' to implement among non-users. Carmichael *et al.* for example, describe a school where the experimental teacher's peers ignored what she was doing until parents initiated a fund-raising drive for microcomputers. Lee (1986) did a follow-up study in four schools during the school year after completion of the initial board-wide in-service cycle. Most teachers in two of the schools were actively using their scheduled times in the microcomputer labs, while teachers in the other two schools were, with the exception of a few individuals, not frequent users. Lee found that the variation in degree of use could not be explained by differences in administrative pressure and support, location of the computer lab, software availability, the computer lab schedule, teacher background (sex, age, prior experience with computers) and students. The main factor that seemed to be contributing to uniformly high use among teachers in a school were school-wide consensus on the importance of NET use for students, and the amount of teacher–teacher collaboration in helping each other learn, in solving facilities and scheduling problems, and in co-ordinating lab use to ensure maximum utilization at all times.

Overall we can conclude that consensus, to the extent it currently exists, can be only superficially meaningful in the absence of experiences with concrete, high-quality usage.

Quality and practicality of the change

Innovations are more likely to get implemented and stay implemented when they result in visibly improved student outcomes. Thus the chances for successful change are greater when the technical certainty of the innovations is already known, and when at least some of the benefits for students are immediately apparent to teachers. If the impact of the innovation is uncertain, its success may depend on careful implementation and monitoring of effects and innovation modification during implementation.

The quality for implementation is also a matter of how 'practical' the innovation seems to the teachers attempting to change. Practical innovations are those that address salient student and teacher needs, that fit well with the teacher's situation (e.g. students, organizational setting, curriculum), and that include or result in concrete *how-to-do-it information*. The practicality of innovations also depends on the trade-off between the personal costs (time, effort, etc.) and actual benefits of getting and staying involved.

Quality and practicality: broad picture

Ministry officials recognize that learning to use new machines and software represents a stumbling block for many teachers. A major thrust of the hardware and software development policies is to make the materials as easy-to-use as possible. The idea is that teachers and students would not have to know a lot about the technologies to be able to use them as learning tools. Until that level of technical sophistication is actually achieved, teachers need to know how to solve minor technical problems or have immediate access to someone who can.

A related issue concerns the continuing variability and incompatibility of existing hardware and software in the school systems. Users can hardly see implementation as 'practical' if they cannot transfer what they learn about using one branch of computer and piece of software to another. The ministry's solution is to attempt to create a situation where machines and software have a consistent environment, i.e. to make the software portable form one machine to another.

While the ministry is doing its best to maximize the quality of software produced for use on GEMS, officials acknowledge a continuing uncertainty about ease-of-use and student impact. Attempts to reduce this uncertainty include the collection and analysis of field test data, dissemination of findings to software developers, setting up a technical assistance centre at the Ontario Institute for Studies in Education (OISE) for developers, and maintaining hot-lines through OESS to identify bugs and problems in software and its use.

This uncertainty surrounding learning outcomes is a focal concern. Ministry officials strongly believe that use of technologies can result in improvements in such things as content mastery, thinking skills, problem-solving skills and student attitudes towards learning. At the same time, they admit that actual learning outcomes of the creative use of open-ended software are not well-in-hand.

Quality and practicality: up close

The teachers' need for practical information on how-to-do-it and how-to-use-it is consistently reported, no matter what types of machines and software are used. Conventional approaches to this dilemma have fallen short. Larter and Fitzgerald (1983) found many teachers unable or unwilling to learn from written material on the screen.

Field data confirm the kinds of issues relating to the 'fit' of NET to local curriculum and organizational conditions. Major constraints can be imposed by local curriculum structures and norms. Carmichael *et al.* (1985) described how teachers' efforts to implement Logo were hindered and even diminished by inflexible timetables and the expectations of other teachers as to what content should be covered when.

The Carmichael *et al.* (1985) study provides the best available information on the problems associated with fitting NET use into the organizational structure of the classroom. They found that teachers who succeeded had to make major changes in timetabling and classroom arrangements on a trial and error basis during implementation. Teachers in that study had considerable difficulty trying to provide individual attention to students on the computers because of class size, especially in computer labs. Some teachers and students had a hard time adjusting to new classroom arrangements which placed students closer to each other and led to more noise and more moving about the room. All in all, it is likely that using NET increases teachers' workload in the short run, as they attempt to sort out the management, instructional and student monitoring problems: counter-balancing the increase in workload is high student and teacher interest and motivation.

In her in-service follow-up study of microcomputer use in four elementary schools, Lee (1986) documented the trials of trying to find or create appropriate space for microcomputer labs. Interestingly, a seemingly good location (e.g. ample space, quiet, non-disruptive of other teachers) did not guarantee high use, and a seemingly poor location (e.g. crowding, noise level, interference with and from other teachers' activities) did not necessarily spell low use. All the schools had trouble finding a suitable location. Lee's data indicate that for lab configurations, facilities problems are to be expected, and how much these problems work against implementation depends on the presence or absence of other factors, for example staff consensus on the priority and need for implementation, and staff collaboration in working out solutions to the problems.

One of the most difficult organizational and individual problems with the practicality of implementation is the consistently reported need of teachers for time to learn what programs can do and time to plan how they might be used. This was documented in all the sources consulted. The current dilemma for teachers is well captured in this quote from an interview with an OISE researcher.

> Not only are teachers busy in school, but computers are busy in school. Teachers don't have time during the school day to work on them. And when they do have the time the computers may not be accessible. The system forces people to learn on their own.

Local conditions

We have just examined the first three factors of Table 2.1, which refer to the nature of the innovation itself. The remaining seven factors refer to the local conditions, procedures and processes that make it more or less likely that continuous attentions and support will be directed to NET prior to, and especially as it is being implemented (see Huberman and Miles 1984; Fullan 1991).

As before, we provide a brief statement to clarify each factor, followed by an attempt to compare perspectives and experiences from the 'broad picture' with those 'up close'.

Central office direction, commitment and support

The commitment and actions of central office administrators are critical to the success of board-wide implementation efforts. General endorsement and verbal support do not suffice. Central administrators have a key responsibility initially to help confirm and clarify the need for change. Implementation is more likely to happen when there is clear consistent communication and pressure from the administration, both initially and during implementation. While there may be latitude for adaptation and variation in use, administrative direction should give priority to the quality not the ease of implementation, otherwise most innovations will be 'down-sized' or adapted away.

Administrative pressure must be accompanied by *assistance*. Assistance requires adequate resources for training, consultative help, release time, materials, etc. throughout the change effort (see factor 6, Professional development). It means targeting these resources on the implementation requirements and on specific problems. It also means establishing clear responsibility for managing and facilitating the change effort at the board and school levels. The seriousness of administrative intent is perhaps most usefully demonstrated when teachers see real efforts being made to identify and resolve problems arising during implementation, and real recognition being given to those who progress in making the change.

Central office direction, commitment and support: broad picture

According to ministry officials, most Ontario school systems have already made a substantial financial commitment to the acquisition of microcomputer hardware and software. One cited a private contractor's estimate that 'school boards would spend over 800 million dollars on information technology over the next ten years even if nothing was done centrally'.

The problem as viewed from the perspective of the ministry, is that there may be insufficient understanding of the full potential of the technology for use in education, a lack of clear policy vision, and confusion in choosing between alternative products and uses. An underlying concern is that the support of school system authorities for NET implementation may be oriented more towards conventional computer literacy and drill and practice type uses than towards the creative use of computers as a personal learning tool across the curriculum.

Apart from making the technology available, and facilitating access to professional development and consultative assistance, ministry officials believe that school system authorities should work on creating a supportive climate for adaptive implementation 'With the new technology there is a need for latitude for risk taking, experimentation, being supportive.' The picture is also one of pressure, but pressure combined with encouragement, support and recognition for trying out different ways of using the innovation. There is a less explicit expectation that school board officials will be receptive to changes in such things as curriculum structure and timetables, classroom organization, teacher roles and pupil evaluation/reporting methods arising from school-level experimentation.

Central office direction commitment and support: up close

The 1982 Provincial Review Report on Instructional Use Of Computers stated that 'most boards do not have policy statements for computers, but many have computer committees that are developing recommendations'. Despite the policy gap, case studies of twelve boards across the province revealed considerable early support from boards for hardware and software acquisition and teacher access to professional development. Central support was typically a response to initiatives undertaken initially by enthusiastic teachers and parents. Where policies existed, the emphasis was more on computer awareness and literacy goals than on using the computer as a learning tool.

In their study of the introduction of microcomputers in Toronto elementary schools, Larter and Fitzgerald (1983) report a pattern of general support from the central office for grass-roots microcomputer adoption and use, without specific policy directions to guide utilization and implementation assistance. Many teachers were frustrated by the absence of clear system-level expectations for microcomputer adoption and use. Individual schools were basically doing their own thing. At the board level several departments were involved with hardware and/or software, but their responsibilities were ill-defined and there was little overall co-ordination of efforts.

To some extent, the lack of local policy directions observed in these early studies has changed given the increase in microcomputers in the schools since 1982. Lee's (1986) description and evaluation of a board-wide computer in-service programme for elementary teachers provides a more recent picture of central office direction and support for implementation. The board invested considerable money in new equipment, support personnel (co-ordinator, consultants) and support materials (manuals) in conjunction with the in-service. Participation was voluntary. Lee attributed the high participation rate (95 per cent) in large measure to administrative pressure from the central office and, in turn, from principals. The director of education made a videotape encouraging teacher involvement. Principals were directed by the superintendent of personnel to indicate that certificates would be placed in the files of teachers completing the course. Additional incentives for teacher participation included offering the course at no cost at their own school, so they did not have to drive anywhere and could learn with their peers.

Much has been said about the importance of administrative latitude for risk-taking and experimentation by teachers using the technology, due to the uncertainty about effective usage and student outcomes. Early field data (e.g. Larter and Fitzgerald 1983; Carmichael *et al.* 1985) indicate that administrators have given relatively free rein to variations in use. Comments from one of the OISE researchers interviewed, however, illustrate that the absence of clear expectations is very discomforting for some teachers.

> Boards want them to just get comfortable with using the technologies. Expectations have been relaxed. But this causes an inner conflict for teachers and stress for teacher. They have no guidelines about what to do. They are not used to operating under no guidelines. Of course, there are some teachers who are exploring and enjoying the chance to take a risk.

Process for implementation and institutionalization

Successful implementation does not just happen. The people organizing and facilitating a change effort must have a *vision of the change process* that is conceptually sound, organizationally practical, and politically sensitive to the local and external context. Above all they have to be able to put together a clear organizational model and set of procedures for achieving implementation and continuation of change. In a very real sense an effective process for implementation is one that explicitly takes into account the other nine factors examined in this section.

Good implementation requires good planning. Plans do not have to be in the form of elaborate documents, but they do need to focus on the right factors and have the approval of people in positions of authority to see that they are carried out.

During the initiation phase, planning should focus on creating an organizational structure and process for the change. This includes setting realistic timelines for implementation and deciding when to introduce it to different target groups throughout the system, as well as determining strategies for such things as acquiring and distributing materials, communicating role expectations, providing initial and follow-up training, consultative assistance, monitoring and problem-solving. It also means establishing a priority for the project and coordinating it with other innovation projects in the local setting.

Effective planning during implementation involves a basic shift in focus from the organizational design for project implementation to the progress, problems and concerns that arise. Good planning at this stage is dependent upon active input and participation of users and front-line managers and facilitators, since they are in the best position to identify the nature and location of problems, and may contribute effective solutions from the field.

Planning for institutionalization is chiefly a responsibility of administrators. Significant changes may be short lived unless attention is given to ongoing budget requirements, replacement materials, training of new personnel, supervisory and support roles and the policies needed to carry on. It is worth noting that successfully implemented innovations often do not become 'mandatory' until they reach the institutionalization stage, once their effectiveness and acceptability has been clearly proven.

The significance of establishing a clear process for implementation can be best appreciated by observing that in the absence of such a process even very high initial enthusiasm on the part of teachers can be squandered. Similarly, early reluctance is often transformed to commitment when supportive procedures are used (see Huberman and Miles 1984).

Process for implementation and institutionalization: broad picture
We did not specifically ask our interviewees what organizational approaches they thought school boards were taking in regards to NET implementation. The pervading sense, however, is one of uncertainty. There is uncertainty at the ministry level as to what an effective school-board-level implementation model and process would look like, and the extent to which boards are, in fact, developing systematic approaches to introducing and supporting the use of microcomputers in schools.

There is a clear perception at the ministry that long-range planning for utilization of computers in education is essentially at the local level. A 1983 Policy/Program Memorandum strongly encouraged school-board-level planning and identified a range of issues which those plans should address, for example educational objectives; curriculum (content, software selection, evaluation, implementation monitoring, integration of OESS materials, etc); computer equipment (current and anticipated uses and distribution, future needs, co-ordination with in-service, integration of GEMS, servicing); administrative support services; implementation strategies and in-service plans; resource requirements and sources of external assistance. A 1987 Policy/Program Memorandum (No. 91) states less equivocally that 'school boards should design and implement system-wide and/or school-based plans that will help teachers and their students to exploit this technology for educational purposes in all appropriate areas of the curriculum'. An Advisory Bulletin distributed with that Memorandum suggests the following basic components of an implementation support system should be included: appointment of curriculum and technical computer support personnel, allocation of teacher planning time, in-service training for teachers in curriculum-based uses of the technology, release time for in-service, resource sharing among boards, dissemination of research findings about use of the technology, communication with parents about integration of the technology into the learning process.

Process for implementation and institutionalization: up close
The field data reviewed for this report do not really give us a good handle on overall local organizational processes for board-wide NET implementation. Studies typically focus on projects involving individual schools or teachers, rather than implementation across the system (Pilot Schools Projects 1983; Carmichael *et al.* 1985).

On the whole, these data indicate that the main focus of planning initially concerns the acquisition and distribution of hardware, deciding on the approach to use in schools (e.g. classroom based, permanent or rotating labs); software development, evaluation and distribution; providing access to introductory computer courses for interested teachers; and creating board-level computer resources positions. The predominant concern is making sure that schools, teachers and students have equal access to available equipment and materials. Boards may offer local teacher training opportunities or facilitate participation in external professional development activities, but the common strategy is to let individual teachers or schools decide on their own approach to professional development. Assistance with microcomputer implementation is being handled much like subject areas of the curriculum, by appointing central resource personnel to assist with professional development and provide consultation on request. It seems safe to say that boards have relied a great deal on in-school expertise for implementation assistance, i.e. the resident experts. This appears less a feature of organizational design, however, than as an adaptation to grass-roots initiative in the schools.

In short, research is needed to find out how boards are organizing support for NET implementation at the system level.

Professional development and assistance

The characteristics of effective professional development programmes are fairly well known. The greatest effects are achieved when explanation of new practices is combined with demonstrations, opportunity to practice in non-threatening contexts, and individual feedback (i.e. 'coaching') back in the classroom. Staff development activities can come in a variety of types – event-specific workshops, meetings, conferences; ongoing consultants, support group meetings, user manuals – and from a variety of sources – external consultants, board consultants, knowledgeable administrators and fellow teachers. Regardless of their identity the providers must be credible to teachers implementing the change, and the activities should focus on assisting with implementation of specific innovations. Staff development during implementation should be oriented increasingly towards implementor level-of-use of the innovation and/or known implementation problems, as opposed to general characteristics of the innovation.

Studies of successful implementation efforts have repeatedly documented the importance of ongoing interaction among innovation users during implementation. Such encounters can provide an opportunity for sharing and joint problem-solving, identifying needs for in-progress of change. Release time for staff development and individual planning is also a valuable form of assistance, particularly during the early stages of implementation when teachers are still struggling with the mechanics of organizing and learning how to carry out new practices.

A critical and often overlooked component of staff development is the need to institutionalize provisions for ongoing socialization and training of new staff members with the use of the innovation.

The impact of quality professional development and assistance during implementation is not just progressive mastery of new practices. The ongoing attention accorded to an innovation helps communicate the seriousness of the effort and can stimulate greater commitment on the part of implementors.

Huberman and Miles (1984) in their detailed examination of twelve case studies summarize the point best:

> Large-scale, change-bearing innovations lived or died by the amount and quality of assistance that their users received once the change process was underway . . . The forms of assistance were various. The high assistance sites set up external conferences, in-service training sessions, visits, committee structures and team meetings. They also furnished a lot of ongoing assistance in the form of materials, peer consultation, access to external consultants, and rapid access to central office personnel . . . Although strong assistance did not usually succeed in smoothing the way to early implementation, especially for the more demanding innovations, it paid handsome dividends later on by substantially increasing the levels of commitment and practice mastery.
>
> (Huberman and Miles 1984: 273)

Such a serious and powerful approach to ongoing professional development and assistance is especially needed in the case of NET given our analysis of the characteristics of the innovation. Of all the factors influencing implementation, professional development (of the type we are describing) is most critical.

Professional development and assistance: broad picture
Ministry officials distinguish different target groups of NET users whose professional development needs vary depending on their positions and prior experience with microcomputers. Traditional user groups, such as computer studies and maths teachers, tend to be interested in computer languages, programming and how computers work, whereas the majority of teachers just want to know how to use the technology as a resource for learning. For teachers who have little or no experience with microcomputers and software, the major hurdles initially are to interest them in the benefits of using the technology in the classroom and to get them comfortable with the mechanics of using the equipment.

For teachers who have overcome the initial attitudinal and mechanical barriers, all ministry sources agree that the main focus of professional development should be to help them learn how to integrate the use of computers and software into the regular curriculum and classroom activity. Major learning needs for classroom use include

- what specific software can do
- how specific software works
- how to integrate the software into the curriculum
- how to use software as an integral part of classroom activity
- classroom organization issues (e.g. facilities, scheduling, grouping, student interaction)
- pupil evaluation methods.

So far the ministry has relied mainly on traditional sources of professional development for teacher training to support NET implementation. The faculties of education are a major source. A computers in education course is now required in pre-service programmes. Other computer-related courses are offered, as well. On the in-service side, the faculties run a three-part Computers in the Classroom programme for the ministry, which leads to a specialist certificate in computers in education. According to one interviewee, this has been one of the most heavily booked additional qualifications programmes in recent years.

TVOntario runs a popular introductory course by television called 'Bits and Bytes'. One of the ministry officials interviewed reported that about 20,000 teachers had registered for that course since it was first offered. Of course, Boards of Education organize and offer in-service workshops and programmes on their own and in collaboration with the Teachers' Federations. New associations of educators committed to computers in education, such as ECOO (Educational Computing Organization of Ontario), hold annual conferences with workshops.

One of the recent ministry projects involves the funding of six 'lighthouse implementation projects' designed to support the establishment of exemplary implementation, and the identification of effective implementation strategies within these sites, which might be disseminated to other boards across the province.

On the whole, it is evident that the kinds of projects and proposals envisioned so far by ministry officials are primarily oriented towards awareness, demonstration and practice at the front-end of implementation for innovation users. Strategies for systematic follow-up support for implementation assistance, at the school and classroom level, are not built into most of these conceptualizations.

Professional development and assistance: up close
Drawing conclusions about the 'up-close' character and impact of NET related staff development and assistance is difficult, due to the lack of detail on this component of implementation support in the field data consulted. What we can do is summarize what kinds of support activities have been going on, identify some major variations in approach, and formulate some impressions of their effectiveness in terms of the diffusion of the technology to new users and the appropriateness of assistance provided.

Early field studies (Larter and Fitzgerald 1983; Pilot School Projects 1983; Carmichael *et al.* 1985) indicate a wide variety of external and within-board sources of initial professional development. External sources include the three-part specialists course, the TVOntario course, university and community college courses, computer user group conferences, training through other public/private organizations, self-instruction materials, family and friends. Sources internal to the boards include invitational courses and workshops, school-specific workshops, continuing education courses and other teachers in the building. Parent volunteers and even pupils are mentioned as sources of teacher training in some schools.

School-level diffusion of microcomputer use appears to be linked to the scope of in-service participation. The Pilot School Projects and Carmichael *et al.* studies indicate lower percentages of use and slower spread to non-users in schools where only a few teachers take part in in-service opportunities. In a study of microcomputer implementation in several school districts in the USA, Yin and White (1984) found that the rate of adoption (the number of machines acquired over several years) was correlated to the presence or absence of group training activities (in addition to individual assistance). Lee's investigation of microcomputer use following intensive school-wide in-service programmes, lends additional support to the view that training teachers in school specific groups is an effective way to stimulate widespread beginning implementation in a board (Lee 1986).

In our view the issue is less a question of quantity than of availability of support at different stages of the change process, i.e. the need for assistance (both in-service and consultative) during as well as at the beginning of implementation. Twelve of the thirteen teachers participating in Carmichael *et al.*'s Logo-use study, for example, already had previous training and experience with computers (half had already used Logo), but received no specialized training or help during the project (except a Logo Users Manual). All the teachers expressed strong needs for additional in-service and consultative support at the curricular and technical levels. As one put it, 'presenting a teacher with the program and the manual and nothing else was like a nightmare'.

Lee's (1986) research on microcomputer use following an introductory in-service for elementary teachers learning to use the DRAW, EDIT and LOGO programs on ICONS, provides another example of the need to structure ongoing support for implementation. The initial in-service combined weekly after school explanation, demonstration and practice sessions (four hours per week, sixteen hours total) with immediate application, adaptation and coaching assistance in the computer lab over a four to six week period in each school. The classes were taught by a board consultant. Computer resource teachers remained on site to help teachers on a daily basis. A training manual was provided as well. Although 95 per cent of teachers at each site participated in the in-service and tried out the innovation with students in the lab, the level of mastery obtained by the end of the initial in-service was modest.

We cannot really comment on the merits and drawbacks of mandatory or voluntary in-service. Personal communications from two of our field sources, however, indicate that because of the emphasis being placed on NET use by system officials (and parents), teachers often think that training is obligatory when offered at the school level. This perception grows when in-service is accompanied by public pronouncements of support from officials, and when it is coupled with access to equipment, materials, release time, consultants, etc. In any case, expectations to use NET are so high that most teachers probably end up wanting or thinking they should use NET. We would venture to say that problems of implementation and associated needs for professional development apply both to enthusiastic and reluctant users. Motivation is no substitute for technical competence.

In-service and practice time are two kinds of help. Access to consultative assistance is another. Local implementation data confirm the need of teachers for ongoing access to knowledgeable and credible computer resource personnel, both for technical questions and problems and for ideas about classroom use. While we know there are increasing numbers of board computer co-ordinators and consultants, data on the actual activities and impact of these people on NET implementation are sorely lacking.

In summary, ongoing professional development is perhaps the most critical direct factor affecting implementation. Carmichael *et al.* (1985: V) for example, found that 'teachers need strong technical, educational, emotional and social support in coping with changes demanded by the creative use of computers'. Teachers' sense of competence and mastery over the machine and software uses is the issue. Professional development must be characterized by access to high-quality software, ongoingness, curriculum and instruction embeddedness, a variety of learning partners (e.g. co-ordinators, other teachers), a variety of learning formats (e.g. visits, workshops, meetings, group, one-to-one), opportunity for practice-practice-practice and feedback, and data on the impact of NET on students.

Implementation monitoring and problem-solving

The success of implementation is highly dependent on the creation of effective ways of getting information about implementation progress and problems from users in the classrooms to appropriate building and central administrators and assisters. While formal technologies for 'evaluating implementation' are available, monitoring does not have to be conducted like research. The crux of the matter is to get the right people talking together about implementation issues on a regular basis. Furthermore, data on student learning and attitudes is needed for a number of reasons including feedback on progress, and at some point information to decision-makers.

Getting information about implementation progress needs to be channelled into provisions for additional in-service and assistance, materials support, and possible modifications in plans, organizational arrangements and the innovation itself – i.e. problem-solving.

Implementation monitoring and problem-solving: broad picture
Ministry sources emphasize the need for careful monitoring of ongoing developments in the NET field and of local implementation in the school system. The need arises from rapid changes in the technologies and continuing uncertainty about alternative products and uses. Present proposals call for a formal overall review of ministry policies, plans and programmes for NET utilization every three years. Here we describe the perspective and approach to monitoring local implementation reflected in our interviews and ministry documents.

Most of the ministry officials interviewed felt their present knowledge about local implementation progress and needs was biased by the fact that most of their field contacts are with committed users, rather than with the majority population of reluctant or non-users.

The rate and pattern of hardware acquisition is being monitored by requiring school boards and schools to include data on numbers and types of microcomputer systems in their annual September statistical reports. Of course, data on the presence of microcomputers in schools reflect only on their availability, not on their use.

One research strategy mentioned earlier is to fund locally designed pilot projects to demonstrate and document classroom uses, curriculum relevance and student achievement, and implementation strategies. Information about these local pilot projects is to be assembled and disseminated to other boards through the ministry. This initiative, known as the 'lighthouse implementation project', will fund six boards up to $170,000 each ($100,000 for GEMS, $70,000 for implementation support).

One of the main vehicles envisioned for monitoring and stimulating implementation is contract research. Microcomputers in education has already been designated a strategic priority within the ministry's contractual research programme. As indicated in excerpts from our interviews, the rationale for research is based on the need to clarify further the actual effects of the technologies on students, teachers and schools, and the most effective ways of using them under varying organizational conditions.

> We need to put research back into the system about the use and impact of these technologies. Research on good applications, good usage, success and war stories need to be fed back into the user network to have an impact as it evolves.
>   We need to allow new models to evolve . . . Observe them . . . Do formative evaluation . . . And then generalize across to large numbers of teachers.

The scenario described presumes a high level of research-based knowledge utilization at the local and provincial levels. It also presumes a high degree of openness to ongoing change in innovation use. From what we know about knowledge utilization in schools, and about the developmental nature of change in practice among teacher, both presumptions are on shaky ground (Hall and Hord 1987).

Implementation monitoring and problem-solving: up close
Most of the field studies at our disposal were examples of the kind of in-house and contract research the ministry typically uses to document what is happening in the school system in relation to priority issues (Provincial Review Reports, Review and Evaluation Bulletins, contract research publications). While they provide important data on many aspects of local NET implementation, none had much of anything to say about how school system officials, central office consultants, or even principals, manage to keep tabs on what teachers implementing the technologies do in the classrooms/labs, and whether information in implementation progress and concerns get somehow fed back into organizational support for the change.

Larter and Fitzgerald (1983) described the situation when microcomputers were first being introduced in the Toronto Board's elementary school. In terms of communications about implementation, it is not a very promising picture. Teachers reported frustration and confusion about 'fuzzy' communications channels in seeking guidance and help from the central office. In one characterization, the researchers described the overall situation as an 'experimental preparedness context'.

> Within such a context, there are few definitive answers: instead dozens of ideas burst forth. Individuals in one part of the system may not know what those in other parts are doing and thinking; individuals at all levels may frequently change their minds about how to use the innovation and much of the evidence regarding the advantages and disadvantages of the innovations is of an anecdotal nature.
>
>   (Larter and Fitzgerald 1983)

According to the authors, individuals at all levels must be 'willing to experiment' in order for this context to exist and be maintained. This image seems to correspond to the ministry view that there should be ample latitude for variation in use initially. What is missing is the second dimension of that view – that information on what is happening, what is working and what is not should be systematically gathered and disseminated with an aim towards building increasingly convergent knowledge about best practices. Instead, we get a picture of 'anecdotal' *ad hoc* knowledge about microcomputer use in education trickling through the informal communications network of routine social interaction.

There is clearly a need for research to document working models for implementation, including the mechanisms created to monitor and use information about implementation progress and user concerns at the school system and school levels.

Principal's leadership

Much research points to the critical role of the principal's support for implementation of educational innovations at the school level (see also Chapter 4). Effective implementation depends on the principal taking an 'active' role in initiating and/or responding to change efforts within the school. Principals who are successful managers of change may be directive or responsive in their approaches, but they cannot just leave the responsibility to adopt and carry out changes to their teachers.

Principals need to be 'knowledgeable about innovation' goals and expected uses in order to understand the needs, progress and problems teachers experience during implementation. While they may choose to undergo training and become users themselves, and to become directly involved in providing teacher assistance, participation at that level is not essential, so long as the principal provides access to resources, training and assistance from others. Research indicates that principals often depend on assistance from a 'second change agent' in the school – e.g. a vice-principal, a key teacher, a central office consultant – especially in secondary schools (Hall and Hord 1987).

Research indicates that effective principals work with teachers to develop shared visions of what the school should be accomplishing for students. They use external innovations as opportunities to further those aims. Overall, the principal must attend to the following components of the change process:

- initial and follow up in-service
- consultative assistance during implementation
- user planning time (during early implementation)
- user interaction and problem-solving
- latitude for risk-taking, errors and gradual mastery of new practices
- protecting users from undue demands
- holding users accountable for the change
- recognizing and rewarding user efforts.

Principal's leadership: broad picture
Policy documents concerning NET implementation have little to say about the role of principals in the process. In our interviews we asked ministry officials to

comment on changes for principals and their needs *vis-à-vis* their expected role in implementation.

Ministry officials generally agree that principals are key agents in the success or failure of implementation in schools, especially at the elementary level. Principals need 'to understand what NET implementation is all about' and 'to be familiar with use of the machines' though they do not have to be resident experts. Most interviewees emphasize the need for principals 'to encourage' teachers to get involved and use the technologies, to be 'flexible' and to encourage 'experimentation' in use, and 'to guide' them towards those practices that seem most effective.

Principal's leadership: up close

In the documents consulted for this report little was actually said about the experience of principals in the initiation and implementation of microcomputer use in schools, although most studies cited the importance of principal support.

In their 1982 study of the introduction of microcomputers into 115 Toronto Board elementary schools, Larter and Fitzgerald (1983) found that principals on the whole were 'less enthusiastic and prepared than many regular classroom teachers'. The newness of the technology and the suddenness of its arrival into the school caught many unprepared. Few had prior experience and many were busy with other priorities. Of course, there were some who were eager to get involved, despite their lack of knowledge, and others who were already computer literate and committed to implementation. One difficulty noted concerned the emergence of resident computer experts in the schools, who frequently took on important responsibilities for co-ordinating computer use in the school and assisting fellow teachers. In some schools this led to confusion about lines of authority and who should make the decisions about microcomputers, particularly when the principal lacked computer knowledge and interest.

In their study of Logo-use by thirteen teachers in nine schools, Carmichael *et al.* (1985) gathered some data on principals' support for project teachers and microcomputer use in general. They found wide variation in principals' personal interest and involvement in learning about microcomputers, active support to teachers, and leadership concerning the general use of computers in the school. Four of the principals attended Logo workshops or general in-service on microcomputer use, in addition to facilitating staff training. Two were non-users, but strongly encourage staff to take advantage of in-service opportunities. Two others showed interest, but basically left it up to teachers to carry out the change on their own. One gave little support and little interest until parents initiated a fund-raising drive. The researchers found that project teachers 'felt more secure trying out new ideas' where their principal gave active support, and that principals' 'leadership in terms of igniting enthusiasms and in drawing out expertise among teachers seemed crucial in the increased acceptance of computers'.

The following list summarizes the kinds of support given by principals in another study:

- leadership on project steering committees
- giving high priority to the project in the school
- facilitating staff development, including provision of release time for training and meetings
- getting early users to train other teachers
- reorganizing school timetables to schedule student access to computers
- ongoing communication with all parents and support for involvement of interested parents
- maintaining open-door policy for visitors
- rearranging facilities to accommodate implementation.

(Pilot School Project 1983)

Community support

Research indicates that implementation of most educational innovations proceeds without much community awareness and involvement. But when community members do take an active interest in the adoption and implementation of particular innovations, their support for or against the change is likely to be a major factor in local decision-making and commitment. In short, if parents actively support the change, boards and administrators are more likely to make it a priority, apply pressure and commit resources, and teachers are more likely to give it a try. On the other hand, active parent opposition can easily thwart implementation, no matter how good the innovation is or how committed school personnel are to its use.

Community support: broad picture

The following quote from one of our interviews with ministry officials captures the essence of how community support for microcomputer implementation is seen:

One thing different about this movement is that it is largely bottom up. There is a spontaneous appreciation in the public of the importance of the technology. The public thinks computers should be in schools and kids learning about them, though maybe not for the same reasons as us. In the face of that interest, teachers feel pressured not to reject. They have to accommodate. That bottom up pressure is lacking in most guideline situations.

Community interest and support, thus, is perceived as one of the major factors contributing to the adoption of microcomputers in schools. Paradoxically, however, that same interest is not necessarily seen as a positive force for implementation of the ministry's goals for use of the technology in schools:

We have to decide what we want kids to learn. And then we have to convince the public that it is learning and that it is worthwhile.

If you can convince parents that the basic content is being taken care of then it would free up time for other things. Many officials and parents still have a 'show me' attitude towards the educational uses of micro-computers.

The concern expressed by these interviewees is that parents may be committed to having their children learn about computers, but it is not clear that they understand what it means to learn with computers. Consequently, the high level of community interest represents a potential problem that cannot be ignored in the implementation of microcomputers as creative learning tools across the curriculum. Ministry planning documents call for expanded com-munication efforts to the public to educate them about the educational uses and benefits of the technology and to gain their support for implementation.

Community support: up close

The field data reviewed affirmed the picture of widespread parent acceptance and support for the general introduction and use of microcomputers in schools (Larter and Fitzgerald 1983; Pilot School Project 1983; Carmichael *et al.* 1985). Larter and Fitzgerald found that 'even parents who do not have a microcompu-ter at home . . . do not use microcomputers at work, and have no knowledge of the machines whatsoever, are still interested for the sake of their children'. Student access to the technology is the most frequently cited parental concern.

The most tangible indicators of parent support are their reported initiation and participation in local fund-raising to buy hardware, and the high level of computer-oriented volunteer work on board-school computer committees and in the classroom (pupil supervision, tutoring, extra-curricular activities). Classroom assistance is more prevalent at the elementary level. Schools have taken advantage of available parent expertise for assistance in introductory teacher training and local software selection and development, as well. Car-michael *et al.* (1985) give a good example of the effects of parent pressure to adopt the technology. Other teachers and the principal in one of the Logo-study schools essentially ignored the efforts of the project teacher until parents took on a fund-raising drive to make sure the machines did not go away once the project was over.

A positive side of parent support is the reported encouragement many par-ents give their children to learn about and use microcomputers. This encour-agement manifests itself in such ways as buying home computers, sending programs from home for kids to work with at school, attending continuing education courses to become computer literate themselves, and the previously mentioned volunteer work.

School system–school strategies to educate parents and gain their support for school-level NET adoption and implementation include involving parents on computer committees, parent night displays/demonstrations, open house pol-icies, parent in-service on school projects, presentations to parent/community groups, communications about school efforts through print and other media, and helping parents get training for themselves. Case studies in the Pilot School Project report suggest that more effective approaches combine various types of parent support generation strategies. Larter and Fitzgerald (1983) caution, however, that because so many parents and teachers are novices in this field, and because central policies about microcomputer use are often vague, the potential for misunderstanding is great.

Environmental stability

The outcome of implementation is susceptible to the influence of changes in the general organizational and social context. Frequent or unexpected changes in administration and project leadership, for example, can have a devastating effect on the continuity of a change effort. Career advancement of key personnel is common, both as a result of opportunistic motives and innovation success.

There is also a great deal of routine shuffling around of principals and support staff in some school systems without much regard for project continuity. It is easy for central administrators to create environmental instability by forgetting about local school context. Other important features of the local and macro-environment include such phenomena as major shifts in government policies, alterations in implementation relevant technologies, demographic changes in student populations, economic trends affecting the availability of funding, and public opinion.

Environmental stability: broad picture

The issues of environmental stability identified in ministry documents and interviews, as might be expected, focus on the macro-environment as opposed to the local implementation context. They include the ongoing transformation to an 'information society', the introduction of additional new information technologies, rapid changes existing technologies, and the long-term stability of funding for NET.

One aspect of unpredictability, of course, concerns the continuing invention of additional electronically based technologies with potential applications for education, such as compact disks, video disks and communications networks. Each new invention carries its own implications for change in materials, practices, beliefs and attitudes in the classroom and school. The instability of the technology arise from rapid improvements in existing products as well as the invention of new ones. One official estimates major changes in technology within the private sector every five years. Some of these changes could make implementation simpler, e.g. reduction in the mechanical knowledge needed to use microcomputers. Others imply modification or replacement of materials and another round of unlearning and learning to use the technology. Increasing sophistication in software design and applications suggest that training in software use will have to be ongoing to keep step with those advancements. The allure of the technology and its potential for education makes it easy to overlook the danger of implementation overload for teachers. And as the software becomes more sophisticated, related pedagogical practices will require more knowledge and skills on the part of teachers.

Despite the push towards a portable software environment, the reality is still incompatible hardware and idiosyncratic software. As one ministry official pointed out, the impact of ministry requirements on the microcomputer industry has its own uncertain implementation context. Manufacturers of systems meeting the ministry's functional specifications, however, are collaborating with the government on this issue.

Funding to support the continued development and introduction of microelectronic technologies in education is another area of potential instability in the macro-environment. The basic view is that education funding in general is in a period of contraction, due to reallocation of government resources to economic restructuring and demographic ageing.

Environmental stability: up close
The field data give some insight into the occurrence and effects of changes in the local or macro-environment for NET implementation on the school. These can be grouped under three themes: instability of the technology market-place, uncertainty of continued funding, and staffing changes.

From the consumer point of view, the microcomputer hardware market is unstable, both in terms of rapid changes in quality and cost as new products are invented and others improved, and in terms of assurances of a continued supply of equipment from particular vendors. According to one of the OISE researchers interviewed, some school personnel are waiting 'to see what else might be available down the road'

On the matter of key staff and turnover, Larter and Fitzgerald (1983) found that help from unofficial 'experts' among elementary school staff members was a key factor contributing to implementation. There was an element of uncertainty about what happens if and when these helpers leave, and the need to ensure that they train other teachers in the school so as to reduce the dependency on particular individuals.

Changes in assignment are common practice in elementary schools across the province due to changing enrolment patterns, promotions, new programme requirements and so on. Carmichael *et al.* (1985) report on the effects of change in teaching assignments on several elementary teachers during beginning implementation with Logo. These changes placed very strong immediate demands on the teachers with respect to additional learning, exploration, and preparation time, which were in direct competition with the demands of exploring how to use the computer technology and Logo in these new settings.

The implication is that principals could provide teachers with a great help during early implementation by trying not to change their teaching assignments (e.g. new grade, split classes, new subjects). Even after they became accustomed to using the technology in one grade level or subject speciality, however, the complexity of switching to another assignment may be more difficult than before, due to the large number of lesson items under development for each grade level.

In summary, a number of macro- and micro-environmental factors affect implementation. Significant discontinuities in the selection of technologies is happening in some settings, with uncertain impact on teachers' attitudes towards beginning or continued utilization. We know that mastering NET initially is difficult enough for most teachers. We can also predict that changes in key personnel in the school (principals, computer resource teachers) and at the board level (computer consultants) will have a negative impact on teachers dependent on their support, if measures are not taken beforehand to diversify the expertise.

Conclusion

My aim has been to use the implementation perspective to analyse what we are up against in attempting to bring about widespread use of microcomputers. In summary, the crucial messages are as follows: for more detail see Fullan *et al.* (1988).

1 Current visions of the potential for NET in education vastly underestimate *how difficult it will be for teachers to implement* the changes NET will require in practices, materials, beliefs, and skills. The tasks of learning about the hardware system, about software, about classroom management, and integration with the curriculum will present teachers with a severe problem of overload; we can expect that it will take a long time before many teachers are engaged in 'quality use'. Furthermore, administrators need to learn a great deal about how to fit NET into the current school organization and how to harness the energies of parents, most of whom are already supportive of NET, at least in principle.

2 The learning task is harder because there are *many uncertainties* about NET. We do not know very clearly what good-quality use will look like, or what the real impact on students will be. So boards, principals and teachers do not have clear guidelines. Furthermore, NET hardware and software are changing and developing continuously. We must invent our own future.

3 Much energy has gone into improving the technical quality of hardware and software. This must be balanced by increasing attention to implementation the *quality of use* by teachers and students in the classroom. We need to devote much more time and energy to the question of 'how to get there'. The identification and spread of *effective practices* is crucial; the emphasis has to remain on the quality not the ease of implementation.

4 The best models of use will grow out of *local implementation*. The strategic ideas in this report are centrally built around the idea of 'backward mapping'. Good implementation must rest on what people in schools are really up against. Thus, the ministry needs to engage local school personnel in an active, collaborative search for the best ways of using NET. Cumulative, shared *learning* about NET is the key process.

5 Continued implementation will depend in no large measure on *early success*, both in terms of teachers' ability to master NET in the classroom, and effects on students' motivation and learning. Thus we need to look carefully at the *impact* of use on the learning and attitudes of students, teachers and parents.

Furthermore, at this stage, we should emphasize quality use in a smaller number of schools and boards, before trying to move to wider diffusion.

6 Success will depend on the presence of well-designed, intense, relevant, sustained *assistance* – training in needed skills, and follow-up consulting and support. It will probably be the major key to doing a good job with NET. It must be carried out by credible people who have used NET in classrooms; they must provide demonstrations, hands-on experience, follow-up practice and coaching – building a critical mass of competent users at the local school level. Assistance should focus on school-level groups of teachers rather than on unlinked individuals. Ongoing administrative pressure to engage in a practice-driven search for effective implementation will also be necessary, but must be accompanied by assistance.

7 The ministry must assume some important responsibilities if its NET policy aims are to be achieved. First, it must supply *direct, active leadership*. The ministry must in effect be saying:

> We are in this together as professionals to develop and implement the best possible practice. The energy and vision of teachers and local administrators are the main driving force. It is a shared quest. We are committed to providing a significant share of development, start-up, support, and dissemination costs. We do not know where we will have arrived in ten years – but we have a central commitment to the quality of our search.

> Second, given the scope of the task, and the resources available for implementation support, the ministry must rely on *capacity-building and multiplier* strategies. It is very important to fund strategies which will have widespread pay-off (such as workshops in implementation skills, the development of local consultants, and the building of networks). Relatively modest expenditures for well-designed strategies can make a real difference.

> Third, there must be steady attention to how the entire enterprise is working, growing and developing. This means creating a strong *steering group* that follows progress carefully and considers next steps. In a real sense, the issue for such a group is not only how specific projects are going, but also building a good *infrastructure* for NET in Ontario. This means a good network for sharing well-developed practices across the province, strong regional centres, a cadre of competent assistance-givers and associations of NET users.

At first glance, the task looks enormous, complex, daunting – just too much. Yet after all, as it happens, it will happen in one school at a time. People in that school – teachers, their local consultants, the principal, students, parents – will be doing what they can do, in their own terms. If what they do is supported, honoured, evaluated and effectively shared with others – in and out of schools – the quality and extent of implementation will be furthered. People at all levels must become preoccupied with 'the implementation perspective' if progress is to be made.

Finally, I should emphasize that the intent of this chapter is not to advocate the implementation of new technologies *per se*. It merely uses microcomputers as an illustration of the issues involved when one considers the implementation of a major educational innovation. The implementation perspective warns us that we need to think through the change process and address the key factors known to impact on the likelihood of success.

3 The School District and Curriculum Implementation

Problems of curriculum implementation in school districts (LEAs) are wide-spread. Tight control or centralization at the district level alienates school people and/or narrows the curriculum. School autonomy or decentralization results in drift or at best small pockets of temporary success that go nowhere (Fullan 1991).

In this chapter I report on a case study of a medium-sized district – which I call East County – that has been comparatively successful in achieving district-wide co-ordination of curriculum implementation.* I first describe briefly the official curriculum model that the district has developed over a fifteen-year period. Second, I examine the 'model as practised', including the identification of key factors affecting implementation. Third, I take up the question of the impact of the model. Finally, lessons and implications for implementation arising from the case study are derived. The purpose of this chapter is not to present East County as an exemplar of district practice. In fact, in light of later implementation work I raise some criticisms of the model in the final section of this chapter. But the case study does illustrate very well the implementation perspective when a district aggressively and explicitly pursues implementation issues.

The official model

The East County Board of Education was formed in 1969 from twelve smaller boards as part of the reorganization in the Province of Ontario, Canada, to larger units of administration. By 1986, the system had 17,500 students in 42 elementary schools and 8 secondary schools with approximately 1,000 teachers.

I will not describe the methodology in detail (see Fullan *et al.* 1986). We conducted a case study, drawing on considerable in-house reports and evalu-

---

* This case study is one of four conducted by Fullan *et al.* (1986).

ation studies conducted by the district. We interviewed six of the eight district level superintendents and assistant superintendents including the director of education (chief executive officer), nine of the ten curriculum consultants, and a random sample of four school principals, selecting also two teachers ($N = 8$) from each school. We also asked the ten curriculum consultants to fill out a questionnaire. Our focus was to describe the curriculum implementation model being used by the district, to obtain interviewees' perceptions of how the model worked in practice, factors facilitating and hindering implementation, evidence of impact, and lessons or implications for future improvements.

In his doctoral dissertation, Jones (1985) characterizes the evolution of East County as follows:

> the planned change process in [East County] could be defined as persistent, reflective problem solving in which the system learned from its trials and developed more sophisticated procedures with this process.
>
> (Jones 1985: 347)

Over a fifteen-year period, the county moved in the early stages from a vague concern about quality, to providing some support assistance, to working on problems of lack of administrative leadership at both the superintendency and principal levels, to the development of procedures, programmes and leadership in the management of innovation.

The formal model

The *Handbook for Curriculum Management* describes the official approach and procedures for curriculum improvement in the system. There are two basic foundations to the approach. The first is the notion of Learning Outcomes Programs (LOP). This starting-point emphasizes that the basis for any curriculum initiative is its relationship to clearly stated goals and expectations for student learning. The second basic conceptual pillar is the idea that the Learning Outcomes will be best achieved by a management framework organized as 'Management by Results' (MBR). The *Handbook* summarizes:

> Very simply, MBR emphasizes the collaborative establishment by personnel at all levels of clear, measurable performance expectations followed by regular review and evaluation. (p. 1)

and

> The curriculum management processes . . . are the result of the recognition from both experience and research literature that curriculum implementation does not happen without careful planning. (p. 3)

The substance of the model consists of a five-stage *Program Implementation Sequence*. The sequence includes procedures to develop, implement, and evaluate programmes. The five stages, all co-ordinated and based on collaboration within and across levels, are

1 the school programme stage
2 field–development stage
3 field–test stage
4 county programme stage
5 East County review stage.

The school programme stage
The process is usually initiated when the Ministry of Education issues a new curriculum guideline. Unlike many boards, which simply introduce the guideline to the system, the starting–point for East County is an *analysis* of the new ministry document. The Curriculum Services Department begins by making an analysis of the document in terms of what it says, what is new in it compared to previous guidelines or existing curriculum in the system, and so on. The major objective 'is to produce a synopsis of the document and its learning outcomes' (p. 6). The method used is for the relevant Curriculum Services Co–ordinator to select, train and manage a teacher committee in conducting the analysis. The analysis is validated by subject teachers and made available for school use. Schools at this stage are expected to review the curriculum in question and make it consistent as far as is possible with the ministry guidelines, although there is no developed county-wide programme at this point. The effects at this stage according to the manual are that some teachers become early adopters, some parts of the programme begin to be developed and can be used in the field–development stage, and the system identifies directions that are consistent with its own goals and with Ministry of Education requirements.

Field–development stage
Curriculum Services co–ordinates a process designed to reach agreement on Unit/Lesson Outcomes. A specific and integrated statement of learning out–comes is developed by a Subject Council or Writing Committee. Members are selected from volunteers according to criteria of knowledge, interest, disper–sion across schools, grade levels, etc. The result is agreement on Unit/Lesson Outcomes, a partial development of materials, and a group of teachers with curriculum expertise (Subject Council members and other validators) who can be used for future in–service training, and who can continue to provide mater–ials for the next stage.

Field–test stage
This stage involves the development of curriculum materials to support the programme, the refinement of the programme through trial use in selected classrooms, and the eventual production of a complete programme for general use. Schools participate by identifying teacher participants and by using the materials. These teacher field–testers opt in only after being introduced to the programme in an initial in–service session. During the field–test period they meet regularly with the co–ordinator and school support staff for ongoing in–service training, sharing and problem–solving. The field–testers also submit

detailed evaluations. Other teachers are invited to participate as monitors; as such they have access to all materials developed and are required to turn to submit detailed assessment. The results as stated in the manual are the availability of a useful programme, a significant number of implementers, and an improvement in the curriculum-development skills of participants.

County programme stage
The product of the third stage is a 'County Program which becomes the official core program that all teachers are expected to adopt and begin to implement'. The programme is declared a county programme by the Administrative Council (all superintendents) on the advice of Curriculum Services, which also presents an associated implementation plan. Principals are advised by superintendents and are expected to incorporate the new programme in their 'goal packages' which are worked out with their area superintendent and reviewed every three months. In the goal packages and related activities, principals are expected to be responsible for the supervision and evaluation of the programme in the school by communicating clear expectations to each teacher, and through the use of an assessment procedure to determine both the degree of implementation of each teacher's programme and the assistance needed to implement the programme more fully. Goal packages, formulated by principals for each priority selected, contain the following components: goals, specific objectives, indicators of success, actions to be taken and (eventually) results. Curriculum Services develops and provides in-service materials and consultative services to meet the needs identified by schools, and it designs programme-evaluation procedures to determine implementation growth and current needs.

East County review stage
East County's review stage 'becomes active when programme-evaluation processes become the main methods by which the school and the system make adjustments and improvements in the county program' (p. 10). There is no automatic timeline for reviews. At the county level, Curriculum Services determines the frequency of reviews depending on the degree of concern, need for information, and requests. Schools also conduct reviews to identify their own needs. Programmes are refined by a reconstructed subject council using the variety of evaluation data gathered during the review.

In addition to the model as outlined, there are policies that outline the role expectations of teachers, principals, superintendents, curriculum support staff, and the director, and documents or handbooks designed to help system staff plan and evaluate curriculum improvements.

The model as practised

I first report on how the formal model operates in practice as experienced by those interviewed. I then identify separately those factors that were seen to facilitate or hinder implementation. In this section I consider how the district staff assessed the model and in the following section I consider the impact of the model at the school level. Recall that virtually all central office staff were interviewed (six superintendents and nine consultants).

Remarkably, in each of the fifteen interviews, we obtained a description of activities and underlying principles that was complete, consistent across interviews, and consistent with the official management model. Virtually everyone defined implementation as the process of putting agreed-upon curriculum priorities into practice, or the process of delivery of new programmes in the school and the classroom. Typical of the interviews one superintendent said:

> We take new documents from the ministry, we analyse, and give schools a quick synopsis. We gather some of our strong people and they develop a document and field test it, and then it becomes county-wide. When a curriculum development comes to a point that it should be county-wide, a co-ordinator works out an implementation plan and submits it to Administrative Council where it is eventually agreed and there is a commitment to it.
>
> The implementation plan identifies actions for people to take – superintendents, principals incorporating it into their goal packages, implementation assistance from co-ordinators and the support team.

A second superintendent noted:

> We stress the use of professional development days. We establish at least two professional development days in addition to the normal instructional days. Principals submit plans as to how they intend to implement a county-wide document. At the elementary level we have made great gains with the principals' use of instructional days and other days as part of an overall plan – that is it's a process not an event.

At the implementation stage another superintendent stressed the superintendent–principal interaction concerning the goal package:

> Principals' goal package – a plan for how to implement environmental studies, for example. We supervise what they set out in goal packages – the latter is negotiated. Implementation may look different in one school than another. Principal ownership is shown in dialogue with the superintendent. The goal package is reviewed four times a year – September, December, February, May or June. In between, we are checking and addressing concerns. We have reached a point that the goal packages are really operational. They are authentic, meaningful exercises and they act as supervising, monitoring, and assisting.

Another superintendent reflects on his overall role:

> My role is to encourage the attitude among principals that curriculum really matters . . . The reality is a principal can be totally overwhelmed with management concerns. Then you have to negotiate a goal package with him. And you specifically focus on curriculum-implementation goals.

The only discrepancy, in a sense, that we found in the model as practised was the reference that secondary schools, for a variety of reasons, were at earlier stages than were elementary schools in using the procedures. Most superintendents agreed that while the system has gone through complete five-stage cycles at the elementary level, the county is at the early stages with respect to secondary schools. According to two superintendents:

> Most of the secondary schools are at the school stage (stage one in the model). The county hasn't put together programmes at the secondary level. In the secondary schools there are literally hundreds of courses. Each is supposed to have a rationale and the proper format. Every programme has to be evaluated on the programme scale on the part of the principal. There have to be some plans, realistic ones to improve the programmes. But the reality is that they only work on two or three programmes at a time.
>
> Leadership, in secondary schools, is not organized. You get scattered leadership – not from department heads. Department heads are unlikely to say, 'OK, help me'. OSIS (the new secondary school policy and curriculum document from the Ministry of Education) has brought leadership to the surface.

Concerning the East County model as a whole, the director of education elaborated on the approach and its assumptions:

> I define curriculum implementation as a development process and linked to evaluation. Development is seen as part of implementation, achieving goals, consensus, direction. Examination of the current state and what we can do – moving to successive proximation, recognizing that evaluation is essential. You have to be clear in the mandate. Getting the front end clear is a tremendous advantage.
>
> The procedures we use are common and known to the system. Everyone expects it to happen and asks 'why not' if it doesn't. The data-gathering process at the beginning is intended to identify needs collectively. It is designed to bring it from the grass-roots and then support it administratively, not force it on people. We say to administrators: 'We need your support and this is what it would look like'.
>
> At the development stage, curriculum co-ordinators submit a proposal to the administrative council. We negotiate information and writing teams right back to the school. The critical thing is the area superintendent knows who is involved, and why, and with what expectations. For example, with release time. We are getting area superintendents and principals to value the activity. You try to establish an atmosphere that collecting information is not an evaluation of them but an assessment for improvement.

While there is system-wide agreement on sets of priorities, the negotiation process between superintendents and principals and staff, with respect to implementation planning, means that at any given time, different areas and schools can choose to focus on different priorities according to their most pressing needs. Thus schools are not necessarily working on the same priorities at the same time.

The nine curriculum support staff members said essentially the same things as superintendents said about the model as practised. For example:

> Development of a programme that results in effective use in classes – that's my definition of implementation.
>
> In this board, curriculum implementation is planned change with evidence that there is real change at the student delivery level. We do try to make sure that we don't just give the appearance of change. There is a sincere effort to actually move towards the ideal . . . There is a definite process of planned change that we stick to.

Another support staff member emphasized the need for consultants to screen requests and to establish criteria and expectations:

> I now say to principals, 'so you want this presentation – for what purposes? Where did the need come from? Can my package meet the needs? Where is it going to go? Are you going to be at the meeting since your presence gives teachers support?'

The other consultants all described the five-stage procedure in detail.

> During the first year of implementation in phase 1 there is in-service which amounts to awareness sessions. In phase 2, there is an analysis at the school level about their priorities, and where they are going to start, plus incremental notions over a two-to-three-year period.

Superintendents also reinforced the planning orientation of consultants:

> Support staff have the right to say 'I am not sure it is right for me to come into the school since it is not clear how you are going to follow up.' With this kind of input, they are putting pressure on the individual school to pay attention to the follow-up and not just have a workshop input. We have only six of these people, and they can't cover all the schools. I tried to legitimize their right to ask these questions and to encourage the principals to think about using them differently, and the support staff do have the right to say no when they don't think the conditions are right.

The consultants' questionnaire confirmed and extended the above findings. We asked consultants to report on a specific curriculum project on which they were working. In addition to providing implementation assistance to teachers, all but one consultant responded that they provide 'a fair amount' or 'a lot' of curriculum-implementation assistance to principals. This represents well over 80 per cent: by comparison, the highest percentage of consultants reporting a similar level of work with principals in the other three cases was 46 per cent (Fullan *et al.* 1986).

We asked about the existence of specific implementation plans in reference to the project on which they were working then. All consultants indicated that

Table 3.1   Factors contributing to and inhibiting implementation: East County

Facilitators	*Obstacles*
1 System commitment and preoccupation with curriculum	1 Teacher capacity, overload
2 Director's commitment	2 Principal's lack of leadership
3 Widely understood, sound and practical procedures	3 Financial resources
4 Leadership at central level	4 Additional demands
5 Increased leadership by principals	5 Complexity of the model
6 Open climate, high expectations, high recognition	6 Role of school board and turnover
7 Healthy curriculum budget	
8 Selective use of external agencies	
9 Persistence and cumulative development	

there were written plans at the central level; nearly all (80 per cent) said there were written implementation plans at the school level for the curriculum in question. In response to the question of whether or not the process used in implementing this was in accordance with the system's model, five of the six who replied said 'completely' or 'for the most part'.

We concluded, based on the interviews and evaluation documents, that there was a high degree of congruence between the model as developed and described, and the model as practised. Indeed, virtually all central office staff reflected a strong internalization and understanding of the workings of the model and its focus on implementation at the school and classroom level.

In the interviews, we asked superintendents and consultants to describe what factors they thought were contributing to effective implementation in their system, and those which they viewed as obstacles. In examining the interview transcripts, we identified a number of themes, both positive and negative. There was a high degree of consensus about the main themes, as summarized in Table 3.1.

Facilitators for implementation

Selective quotes illustrate the more specific meaning of the factors.

System commitment and preoccupation with curriculum

> There is a tremendous commitment to curriculum delivery over the last six years in our system.

> You can't get promoted in this system unless you are a programme leader. We have an area superintendent retiring, and the people rumoured as contenders are all programme leaders.

Director's commitment

The director is seen by this system as being on top of curriculum. He sets the tone and this is very important.

The director emphasizes, and we agree, that the primary aim is instruction in the classroom. We try to fulfil that aim. It's a worthwhile purpose, but my God it's hard. This director and the previous director emphasized instruction as the *raison d'être*.

Widely understood, sound and practical procedures
At one level, people referred to the effectiveness of the total model.

The framework is a strength because it leads to planning and steady monitoring of progress. It helps teachers and principals tie it all together. That's the major strength of West County. The consistency. The organized approach.

The close coupling of curriculum development, evaluation and support.

The focus is on help, on assistance; we are clear that teachers need a period of low-risk practice. It's OK not to do something well at the beginning, but it's not OK not to progress to higher levels.

Teachers and principals are more comfortable and feel helped, because the process we have now for curriculum implementation involves them from the beginning and then phases in change. It's more dynamic now. All sorts of feedback loops.

At a more specific level, those interviewed stressed particular components like the principal's goal packages, quality of curriculum, the evaluation process and the importance of the review stage.

The principal's goal package forces them to act.

We have very sophisticated, very good curriculum documents and materials, excellent curriculum development.

A key is the review cycle, as it really does make a difference – people listen very carefully about problems, and we develop strategies, materials and in-service in responding to the reviews.

Leadership at central level

High level of skills in the development group and team approach between administration and curriculum services.

One of the things about [East County] is that people are conceptually in tune with the ideal. I spend a lot of time talking with the Curriculum Services Co-ordinator to make sure I have the ideal perfectly assimilated. The beauty of it all is that all our co-ordinators and consultants sing the same song. They are conceptually consistent.

The superintendents are really skilled in helping principals develop their plans. Our system has done a lot in helping administrators in curriculum management.

Increased leadership by principals
(See also Obstacles to implementation.)

More principals see instruction as a major component of their role.

The level of functioning of the principal. The principals is a major factor. Three of the eleven principals I work with are great.

Open climate, high expectations, high recognition

An open climate where you can discuss, raise issues. A strong problem-solving capability – willingness to look at things. Expectations are clear and high, and there's stimulation and satisfaction.

Another major factor is the incentives and rewards philosophy. There is an encouragement for teachers to work on curriculum-and-review teams, or to get and dialogue with people outside the system.

The chances of good work going unnoticed are very slight. We want people to know if they put out 100 per cent that they will get recognized. It is personal; it is planned. It has recognition and appreciation.

Healthy curriculum budget
(See also Obstacles to implementation.)

Healthy curriculum budget. $100,000 for supply teachers. More than other boards.

We buy a lot of materials and develop many materials. Teachers don't have time to develop materials or to fight to get equipment.

Cost issues – if only one-shot efforts are made, the money goes down the drain. Therefore, put resources into a plan – part of our job is to sell this to the board.

The board consistently supports the programmes in terms of people and budget. The have not done the minimum. They have gone beyond the call of duty. There's a pride in what we are doing.

In the survey, eight of the nine consultants 'strongly agreed' or 'agreed' with the statement that 'the board allocates the resources (money, staff, time) to carry out the school system's approach to curriculum implementation'.

Selective use of external agencies

Lots of contact with the ministry, if I think they have something to use. We look for resources and for information – more at an administrative level. At the regional level they don't have the in-depth knowledge.

We encourage the ministry to come in and evaluate. We co-ordinate it centrally. We try to expand their terms of reference to add questions we want . . . We have learned to be up-front with the ministry, and they are receptive, but they do not want to go as far as we are in being specific. . . . We welcome partnership with the ministry, but there seems to be a reluctance and a certain distance that they want to maintain.

A great deal of contact with OISE [Ontario Institute for Studies in Education] in problem-solving skills. We go to them for the substance. Ken Leithwood (OISE central) and John Ross (OISE field centre) are important here.

Persistence and cumulative development
(See also Obstacles to implementation.)

We have recognized, I think, the need for the organizational conditions and the individual needs to be integrated. The stages we have gone through as a system, and with the leadership we have had, has contributed in a developmental way. There is a value-added development over the three directors.

We are always grooming future leaders – vice-principals for example.

The questionnaire data again confirmed the findings about positive factors. Using the high standard of 'strongly agree' on a four-point scale, 67 per cent strongly agreed that 'this board attaches a high priority to curriculum implementation', and 78 per cent that 'the purpose and goals of the approach to curriculum implementation . . . are clear'.

On the difficult task of effecting 'co-ordinated interaction among senior officials, curriculum support staff, principals, and teachers', 22 per cent strongly agreed and the remaining 78 per cent 'agreed'. Co-ordination among support staff, through regular communication in planning and scheduling assistance in schools, was similarly high (five of eight (63 per cent) indicated that there was regular co-ordination compared to a high of 21 per cent in the other three cases).

Obstacles to implementation

The six categories of obstacles are similarly illustrated in the following quotes.

Teacher capacity, overload

Capability of teachers to keep on top and be knowledgeable about programmes. We have some very sophisticated, very good documents. The more skilled teachers integrate the learning experience across the curriculum. It requires a conceptual skill to oversee the programme. It is not mechanistic, even though we have it as a technology.

Resistance to change in some teachers, despite the number of years we have been in the learning-outcomes process. Now the problem is more at the secondary level, because 'learning outcomes' has grown up in the elementary system.

Principal's lack of leadership

If you have a principal who doesn't place a high degree of importance on curriculum, that's a barrier. If there's not a strong feeling that it matters then you don't get the persistent effort. You don't get the monitoring that goes with planning.

I would say 50 per cent of the principals are involved at a superficial level. . . . The very active principals would be about 10 per cent who have negotiated a plan of identified resources. The rest are not involved.

It is kind of threatening for a principal to realize that his staff is way ahead of him on some things – we need to support those principals with careful placement and professional development.

A major problem at the secondary level is the role of the department head. He is not seen as a programme leader.

We have given principals good directions, but not in-depth training.

It is difficult to draw conclusions about the role of principals, because the standards of those interviewed were very high. Our own approximate conclusion from the interviews is that about 10 per cent were functioning at a very high level – problem-solving in Leithwood and Montgomery's (1986) terms – another 40–50 per cent at the programme-management level striving to get better, and the remaining 40–50 per cent at less than management level, although many were clearly seen as developing towards high levels.

Financial resources

Too few people to do too many things. There has been a cut in support staff.

Lack of resources. We have relatively good financial support, but we need more resource people.

Additional demands

External factors that we can't control.

The day-to-day problems that can't be avoided usurp things if you are not problem-focused . . . Co-ordination of curriculum is not the problem. Co-ordination of everything else is.

Complexity of the model

It is viewed as a complex set of procedures – too complex. It is sometimes viewed as too theoretical. There is complexity as to how the parts relate to the whole . . . The major obstacle with some teachers is that they don't value it – they don't see it as helping them. It's too ambitious and there's too few resources. And the board is saying there's too many resources.

When I recognize what we would have to do to do all this properly, plus how we are ideally set up, plus how far we have come, but how far we have to go, I get discouraged.

Role of school board and turnover

In the political area, trustee turnover, financial cuts, and having to re-educate new trustees.

In summary, it can be noted that some of the factors appear in both lists, such as the role of principals and resources. These are not inconsistencies because the same people who were interviewed talked about the strengths and weaknesses of the system in reference to progress in the development of principals' roles and the pros and cons of the budget.

Impact

In the larger case study we examined the implementation at the school level involving a specific curriculum programme in Environmental Studies (Fullan *et al.* 1986: ch. 7). As well, evaluation studies conducted by the district reported classroom and school-level implementation across the system for the Environmental Studies programme. It is not the purpose of this chapter to report in detail on specific implementation outcomes. A district study in 1984 measuring classroom implementation found that 30 per cent of the eligible teachers were implementing the Environmental Studies programme at a very high level, 37 per cent at a medium level, and 33 per cent at a low level. These results are interpreted by the curriculum co-ordinator as first reflecting considerable progress in that they have moved from a very low percentage to a much higher percentage in implementing a very complex multi-disciplinary innovation in Environmental Studies, and second, that the results revealed that much more focus was needed on front-line implementation. Three main recommendations or strategies were made based on the study:

1 that curriculum services provide differential support and in-service training according to different levels of implementation needs
2 that in-service training for principals be provided
3 that the Administrative Council (consisting of all superintendents) consider how to support and monitor the programme.

After these measures were implemented a follow-up review was conducted a year later (1985). The results indicated that 40 per cent (compared to the previous 30 per cent) were now implementing the programme at a very high level, and pointed to further support action that should be taken.

In commenting on the 1984 review the curriculum co-ordinator made the following observation:

> It alerted the whole administrative group about the possible gaps between perceived and actual degree of implementation. That was a bit of a shock for them. They were expecting more than they saw, given the positive side, too, since we began with nothing . . . Now expectations are totally visible and known.

In our study, we selected four schools at random and interviewed the four principals and eight teachers (two from each school). We used the Environmental Studies programme as an example in order to give the questions a concrete reference point. Factors identified as facilitating the implementation of Environmental Studies were as follows (maximum number of mentions = 12):

- the principal, including the use of plans or procedures   (12)
- ongoing in-service   (11)
- teacher–teacher contact   (9)
- curriculum consultant support   (10)
- good programme and resources   (10)

Obstacles to implementation were mentioned less frequently but included difficulties of 'covering' all the material, the complexity of implementing and measuring higher-order skills, the need for more in-service on teaching strategies and better implementation planning at the school level.

I return to the larger question in assessing what the overall impact of the model has been. There are basically two aspects to this question. First, what is the extent and quality of implementation of the model; not an unimportant question since 'implementing the implementation model' is probably more basic and more difficult than implementing particular curriculum innovations (Fullan 1985). The second set of effects concerns the impact or consequences of using the model. In particular, what is the impact on the professional skills of individuals (e.g. teachers, principals), on the institutional development of schools and school–district relationships (e.g. school-level planning, school–district priority setting and follow-through), and on student learning and achievement.

Most of the respondents reported that the model itself was definitely being put into practice by more and more people, and that there was clear progress as it both spread and became embedded more deeply in the procedures of the system. Most stated that the use of the model was benefiting the system, including the administrators, teachers and students. We asked those interviewed to describe the indicators what they saw as evidence for these claims.

Superintendents reported as follows:

> The indicators of success? Are the core aspects being incorporated? Looking for principals' information that he has available, such as a copy of the plan, the dates of visits, student performance, sample units from teachers. I look for specifics, for activities . . . Principals' use of time would be

another indicator. How much time is spent on teacher evaluation? What activities? How much follow-up? What professional development emphasis is the school involved in? Which schools were asking for reprints from the library?

The math K – 8 program. We are gathering new data. We will have data from five years ago, three years ago, and now. We are building a performance-monitoring system. It may tell us something in our Grade 5 programme should be in Grade 4 or in Grade 6, and we should be able to improve programme delivery because of the longitudinal monitoring we are doing. The interviews with teachers and performance tests. We look for individualization in the classroom and for an emphasis on problem-solving and thinking skills . . . We have noticed in these interviews much more awareness on the part of teachers and much more explicitness about what it is they are doing and why.

On the formal realm student results. We have, or are developing, tests which measure this. Sometimes we look at levels of use to measure implementation. Informal indicators are the hive of activity – the meetings of teachers, drawing on our resource centre, materials generation. The co-ordinators give feedback as well. A host of checks and balances. . . . We use evaluation process very formally and very openly to the board and back to the school.

Co-ordinators and support staff said much the same. One co-ordinator stated the progress in a kind of backhanded way:

There has been significant achievement at the school level which could be said as principals would not deny that they have a programme responsibility.

And others:

The review stage is where there is a real impact. There is no doubt that the system has an improved capacity to solve problems at this point . . . We have special programmes out there that fit the outcomes. It's all integrated. One might see integration as an aspect of institutionalization. There are multiple supports for continuation of programmes.

I look for things I didn't see five years ago. For example, I look for teachers with goals. When I see a well-planned, goal-based programme that they can be articulate about, I'm seeing change . . . I see a lot more of that now. I also look for things being internalized. For example, if I hear a principal saying, 'Why, this kid hasn't even been tested yet', I know that change has happened, because now the principal is thinking about testing as a natural thing to do and the ideal thing to do. It didn't used to be that way.

I can tell it is working well by the repeat turn-out of teachers involved in development, and also they bring in samples of what they have been working on for sharing and discussion with the other teachers. We have very few dropouts as we go, even though they are evening sessions. And they are sharing . . . I see teachers starting to get in touch with each other. Teachers are calling and telling me, they are not waiting for me to do the communication.

Another lesson concerns money. We have been able to use the procedures to argue for budget. We have been able to institutionalize a regular budget. It used to be *ad hoc*. The trustees just accept it now.

Because of the success of the evaluation process, it is becoming clearer, more trusted; and people have more confidence. It is another example of how things are coming together. I am very optimistic when I look back five years. I feel very positive of the direction. I guess we are reaping the benefits of things that were planted ten years ago with learning outcomes, or five years ago.

In the survey data, eight of the nine consultants indicated that the system's approach to curriculum implementation was 'very effective' or 'moderately effective' (on a four-point scale). Only one consultant said it was 'mildly effective', none said 'not very effective'. The same number agreed that the system's approach had 'resulted in the professional growth and development of teachers', and that it has had 'a positive impact on teacher–principal interaction' and on 'their interaction of school and central office personnel'.

What then, can we say about the overall effectiveness of the East County Model? Basically, we think it is too early to be definitive, but there is a number of very positive interim indicators: comprehensive procedures are in place; virtually everyone we interviewed could describe the procedures and was clear about expectations; most of those interviewed were detailed in describing how the procedures were followed; most again pointed to a number of specific benefits of the model compared to the situation five years ago; a complex programme in Environmental Studies was started from scratch and has achieved a high level of implementation among 40 per cent of the eligible teachers. Other reviews in maths and Special Education describe additional accomplishments. Above all, highly committed curricular leadership is being increased at all levels (vice-principals, principals, department heads, consultants, superintendents, the director), which has already reached a critical mass, and which is increased with each new appointment. The message and practice are clear: if you want to be promoted in this system, you have to have already demonstrated programme leadership and be committed to, and skilled in, programme-implementation procedures.

There are two reasons why we think it is too early to draw firm conclusions. First, the full-blown model was developed piece by piece over the last ten years so that it has only been in operation in a reasonably complete way over the past three years or so (it is still not complete). For example, the role of the principal has been attended to in an intensive way only since 1983. And the procedures have been used until very recently, mostly at the elementary level, not at the secondary level. Moreover the criteria of promotion means that more and more leaders with an implementation perspective are being added. One would expect that this critical mass of new leaders will make a substantial difference in direct and indirect ways.

Second, more work needs to be done on developing and integrating measures of student achievement into the basic procedures – a task which is receiving priority at the present time. Even here, however, considerable progress on student achievement has been made. The model itself starts with and focuses on 'learning outcomes'. This explicit focus is part and parcel for the model at all stages. In reviewing the case draft our liaison contact person had this to say:

> The process of developing agreement on the 'outcomes' for students in programmes brought a clarity in learning directions which was not present before. Consequently, when teachers are 'implementing the programme at a very high level', the assessment, by [East County] definition, means that they can now demonstrate student-learning growth on a defensible growth scheme. These new capacities for teachers impact directly upon their students.

Ten years of hard work, with at least five more years to go to get the promise of a fully functioning effective model in place in a medium-sized system, may seem like an unacceptably long period of time. Yet these are the messages coming from the implementation perspective. In fact, of course, the work is never completed; it is continuous. However, once there is a significant increase in the basic *capacity* of the district to address priorities and implementation, we expect that managing change on a continuous basis will become more feasible.

Lessons and implications for implementation

I derive two aspects of implications for implementation. The first relates directly to what East County personnel respondents saw as the main issues. In the second aspect I identify the main themes in the context of the research literature.

We asked respondents the following question late in the interview: 'As a result of your experience over the last couple of years or so, what have you learned to do, and learned not to do in introducing change more successfully?' Respondents spontaneously identified with the question. Typical of the observations in East County were:

> I have learned first to involve strong teachers. I have become committed to a model of planned change that requires and gets the commitment of superintendents. Area superintendents are now directly involved in implementation.

> If I have learned anything it is to be slower off the mark so that we have good information to share with people. For example the collection of information around current status by asking teachers who are teaching the

courses. Rather than launching into implementation, we get data and realize that we have to address it collectively rather than as individuals.

We start with the level where people are at. We negotiate with them what they are doing and why. For example, we ask a principal how a particular presentation will fit into an overall plan. Another point, we always work through authority.

In summary, the following factors received a number of mentions:

1 Set manageable expectations – change takes time – but be persistent; focus pressure on a few projects.
2 Build in-school leadership capabilities by developing principals, involving other lead teachers and consultants.
3 Place more emphasis on implementation by avoiding one-shot workshops, preparing for implementation and concentrating on ongoing in-service training.
4 Give latitude for adaptation in schools by accepting variation but maintaining follow-through.
5 Work on people's understanding of the purpose, expectations, and the processes of change.
6 Help teachers fit the innovation into what they already do by clarifying similarities as well as discrepancies.
7 Teachers need concrete curriculum documents.
8 Give teachers the chance to work through a change by encouraging risk-taking and sharing.
9 Build in involvement and support of line administrators.
10 Gather data on extent of implementation and problems encountered, only if there is a procedure for using the data to bring about improvements.
11 Provide incentives, good documents, opportunity for sharing, in-service training, recognition for good work.

As we turn to the themes in the recent research literature, a number of points stand out. First, East County, despite its success, is still very much driven by a system-wide model. Such centralized planning and co-ordination is probably not the solution in the long run for complex multi-level systems. In fact, the key planners in East County acknowledge that their model has not yet fully evolved. As the capacity at the school level develops, these planners expect (and already see) that individual schools will take much more initiative and control over the process. Second, there is not much research available on the role of school districts and the district–school relationships. We are operating in somewhat of a research vacuum on this topic. Third, there are a few recent research studies beginning to emerge (Louis 1989; Coleman and LaRocque 1990; Fullan 1991: ch. 10). In successful cases – where districts and schools are working effectively to implement school and classroom improvements – neither centralization (district controlled) nor decentralization (school-based) dominates. Rather the pattern of success involves continuous two-way negotiation, and mutual pressure and support between individual schools and the district.

In the East County case, I identify ten themes consistent with these developments:

1 From innovations to systems
2 The unknown role of the secondary school
3 The integration of curriculum and professional development
4 The integration of authority and support
5 School-level and district-level co-development
6 Teacher involvement and incentives
7 New roles for consultants
8 Criteria for promotion to positions of authority
9 Longitudinal development of the elements of planned change
10 Capacity building: skill in doing.

From innovations to systems

The most important and overriding theme is that our study directs the focus of concern away from the implementation of specific innovations towards organizational or system approaches to programme improvements as an ongoing component of school system operations. This represents a fundamental shift away from the preoccupation with specific innovations towards a preoccupation with system procedures as the major means for implementing any number of particular innovations. School boards are in the business of managing multiple potential changes simultaneously. Research has been limited because it has been governed by a focus on the implementation of specific projects.

The unknown role of the secondary school

Most of the experiences in East County have been with the elementary panel. We cannot generalize from our study to secondary schools. It is only very recently that the first tentative moves have been made with secondary schools. We have no doubt that not only will many of the same principles of change apply, but also there will be differences. The management of change in large secondary schools is a much more complex affair involving the development of a larger leadership team consisting of principals, vice-principals and department heads, few of whom have had experience let alone training in the direction planning and implementation of curriculum change (for recent examples of secondary school reform see Wilson and Corcoran 1988; Fullan and Newton 1989; Fullan 1990a; Louis and Miles 1990).

The integration of curriculum and professional development

The days of the one-shot workshop at the local level are numbered. Several consultants said, 'I will never do a one-shot workshop again'. By that, they mean that whatever workshops they do, follow-through must be built in, that is they must form part of a plan. Consultants were too pressed for time to waste it. Put in more thematic language, professional development must become more curriculum- and job-embedded. It works both ways: when contemplating a curriculum priority, build in some ongoing professional development; when contemplating a professional development event, link it to curriculum priorities and follow-through (see Little 1989).

This is not to say that large-scale annual conferences, university courses and the like are useless. They serve different purposes: awareness of new ideas, a chance to meet peers, individual learnings, a time to get away from the daily grind. These are valuable and necessary. However, when it comes to local-level curriculum priorities, professional development defined as the sum total of formal (e.g. workshop) and informal (e.g. peer interaction) learnings experienced by teachers and others, must be incorporated as part and parcel of an implementation plan.

The integration of authority and support

Traditionally, in school systems there has been a tendency to keep authority and support separate on the grounds that the evaluative role of authority is incompatible with providing developmental support. Our case study indicates not only that these two functions can be compatible, but also that it is essential that they be closely integrated. In particular, putting the responsibility for implementation planning explicitly and squarely on the shoulders of those in line positions – principals and area superintendents – makes it necessary for support and authority to be combined in a way that greatly strengthens the likelihood that sustained attention will be paid to implementation and follow-through.

Some structural reorganization should also be considered by school boards in reference to this theme. At a minimum, it means making explicit the implementation-planning role expectations of operations superintendents, and moving resources from the district to the school level to support implementation. Beyond this, boards should examine to what extent their present structures facilitate or inhibit the co-ordination and integration of curriculum development, professional development, curriculum support (i.e. consultants), curriculum implementation and evaluation.

School-level and district-level co-development

Researchers and practitioners alike have thought of school-based curriculum decision-making and central-office curriculum decision-making as if they were mutually exclusive. Grass-roots versus top-down, decentralization versus centralization, or whatever distinction one selects are false dichotomies in our case study. Development at one level in the absence of development at the other level is ineffective for accomplishing improvement. Neither grass-roots nor top-down approaches work by themselves. Central co-ordination, pressure and development are essential, but so is corresponding school-based development on the part of principals and teachers as implementation decision-makers. The solution is neither more nor less centralization, but rather it lies in the area of increased interaction and negotiation between schools and area or central offices, and investment in the development of capacities at both levels.

Teacher involvement and incentives

Teacher participation and incentives for becoming involved in efforts at change is a perennial problem. Systems have tried high involvement (e.g. teachers responsible for curriculum development) and low involvement (e.g. curriculum consultants developing curriculum), both to no avail. The best approach in general terms involves setting up a process which starts where people are. This was one of the main lessons learned and emphasized by the people interviewed; it is necessary to find out where teachers are in relation to proposed new changes before launching into a project. In addition, the process is open from the beginning; it involves (i.e. mobilizes) more and more teachers at each stage so that, by the time curriculum reaches system-wide approval, there is commitment and considerable implementation already (that is implementation should be conceived as something that starts right from the beginning when a document is first discussed, or when development commences); the process also provides co-ordinated support and pressure from principals, superintendents and consultants; and finally it is based on a philosophy and practice of recognition through incentives and rewards to teachers at all stages of the process.

The critical question is 'What is in it for teachers if they are to take a new curriculum initiative seriously?' We have seen in the process of change that the early stages of implementation involve great effort (costs) on the part of teachers and provide few tangible benefits. Furthermore, in the experience of many teachers, previous attempts at curriculum change have not been highly positive experiences, that is the costs in time and energy have far outweighed the rewards. Indeed, many of these efforts failed to achieve any substantial results. Therefore, any approach to curriculum change with teachers must reduce some of the early costs and increase some of the early rewards.

New roles for consultants

The role of system consultants is shifting from being technical experts in the content of curriculum (although this will still be essential for specialists) to being experts in the process and procedures of managing change. This applies both to those consultants with essentially curriculum-development responsibilities, and to those whose primary responsibility is professional development. It is a matter of increasing the in-school, follow-up role of those in traditional curriculum-development roles, and of linking the support of professional-development consultants more closely to curriculum-implementation processes.

In any case, consultants will need to combine and integrate expertise in curriculum and in their change process. The latter includes knowledge, commitment and skill in implementation planning, knowledge of how people learn and consequently of the most effective in-service education designs, ability to develop technical aids for the process of change (e.g. to assess implementation, to evaluate progress, to provide guidelines for developing implementation plans), and the ability to participate in, and help principals and teachers develop, school-level implementation plans.

Consultants, as we know, are not trained even for their curricular roles, let alone the change-related aspects they face. In the survey, we asked consultants how useful they found certain experiences in preparing them for their present positions. Of the experiences they found 'very useful', 88 per cent indicated 'on the job experience', 54 per cent said 'attendance at conferences', 37 per cent indicated professional journals, 25 per cent said university courses. Only 13 per cent said 'board-sponsored training'. Consultants, then, learn their skills incidentally. More preliminary and on-the-job in-service training in the process of change is required, if curriculum consultants are to be effective (see Ross and Reagan 1990; Saxl *et al.* 1990).

Criteria for promotion to positions of authority

One of the most common and powerful themes was the recognition and endorsement by everyone that 'if you want to get anywhere in this system you have to have already demonstrated curriculum leadership and skills'. It was most explicit in a recent East County document listing the criteria that would be used in promotion interviews for department heads, but the emphasis on curricular strengths permeated the systems in reference to appointments of vice-principals, principals, department heads and supervisory officers. Combined with the predicted high turnover rates of administrators (in the range of 40–60 per cent in most school systems in Ontario) because of the retirement pattern during the 1990s, we can expect an enormously powerful impetus for managing and supporting curriculum improvements. Another feature of this development will be the appointment of a large number of women, as there is a greater pool of women who have begun to enter the first levels (e.g. vice-principals) and because, in our experience, women tend to be curriculum-oriented (see Fullan 1991: ch. 8; Fullan and Hargreaves 1991).

Longitudinal development of the elements of planned change

Taking the new paradigm – establishing the capacity of school systems and schools to manage multiple changes – it is clear that this cannot be done all at once. In general, it takes persistence, reflection and action. At a more specific level, it can be seen as a process of incrementally putting in place each of the major elements of an effective model of change: initiating central-office procedures; clarifying objectives; doing high-quality curriculum development; attending to the implementation-planning, supporting and monitoring roles of area superintendents and principals; developing one technical aid after another; getting more effective at arranging ongoing, cumulative in-service education for teachers, principals and others; figuring out how best to build in believable, usable programme reviews and other evaluations. The order of these tasks is not the point, but the idea that you can start in any number of different ways, that you cannot do everything at once, and that it takes several years to get the major pieces in place and functioning in a co-ordinated manner is critical. East County has been actively developing its model for at least ten years, and the model still requires further development.

The main reason change takes several years is not the absence of technical knowledge, but essentially because, for a system 'to get good at change', it must go through the process of intense and high-quality implementation of the model. It is not the model on paper that counts, but the degree to which staff at all levels master the skills, co-ordination and internalization (full understanding and commitment) required. This takes time and care, by definition, no matter how wise the approach.

Capacity building: skill in doing

People get better at planned change by doing it, by starting somewhere, and building on it deliberately as they discover aspects that need work. Being a critical consumer of the research on planned change is also an important resource for developing, checking, modifying, and being reassured of the soundness of the approach that is being used. We found evidence that the model being developed attempted to combine research knowledge about effective approaches to change with practical knowledge gained from experiences in applying the models.

As we stated above, the precise order of the tasks is not as important as realizing that one cannot do everything at once. 'Start small, think big', as one of the leading researchers in change advises (Miles 1986). Our own previous recommendation is similar:

> The question of where to start is crucial, but the answer is by no means clear . . . the effective superintendent looks for a number of leverage points, depending on the conditions, and employs several simultaneously – working with principals, professional development of teachers, figuring out ways of maximizing interaction, creating commitment – in short, establishing a number of footholds, promoting them incrementally in mutually reinforcing ways in an attempt to generate school improvement. The advice is to start small and expand as one gets better at the change process through experience in a particular setting.
>
> (Fullan 1985: 418)

The preceding nine themes are interactive and mutually reinforcing. As a set, they amount to capacity building. Once a number of key elements are in place, one begins to reach a critical mass in which actions feed on each other and become more efficient and more effective and the system in a sense comes to have its own generative power. Capacity building is a process whereby reflective practitioners in a system collectively accumulate and organize wisdom about the dos and don'ts of implementation. If done deliberately, with each particular cycle, people get a little better at it, having learned that some things work and that others don't. After several cycles one's theory of change and associated skills and judgement starts to become internalized. Implementation, in a word, becomes easier. While implementation in the future should become less onerous and more gratifying, following the themes identified in this chapter, we should not underestimate the inherent complexities, dilemmas and unpredictability in the business of change. Change must contend with individual personalities, situational conflict, lofty goals and insufficient resources. We are in the business of making progress in the face of perennial problems. As with most complex endeavours, the hardest thing is to get started. The second most difficult thing is to be persistent. School districts do not have a good track record in these regards. Focusing and staying focused on the implementation perspective is central to future success.

4 The Role of the Principal and School Improvement*

The school improvement perspective is also valuable in examining particular *roles*. The principal has often been cited as a key figure in blocking or promoting change, and as such represents a fertile ground for considering the concept of implementation in action. First I review briefly research which singles out the principal as a primary agent of change. Second, I consider new conceptions of leadership that enable us to go beyond the limited finding that principals influence implementation of given innovations. Third, I recommend ten guidelines of action consistent with this new, more powerful conception of leadership.

The principal and change

In the first major study of innovation involving almost 300 school districts, Berman and McLaughlin found that 'projects having the *active* support of the principal were most likely to fare well (1977: 124, original emphasis). They claim that the principal's actions (not what he or she says) carry the message as to whether a change is to be taken seriously and serve to support teachers. Hall and his colleagues (1980) state it flatly: 'The degree of implementation of the innovation is different in different schools because of the actions and concerns of the principal' (Hall *et al*. 1980: 26).

The image of the principal in the research and policy literature has shifted since the early 1980s from the principal as 'gatekeeper' to the principal as 'instructional leader'. Planned change, school improvement, effective schools and staff development all bear the mark of the principal as central for leading and supporting change.

We know rather definitely then, that when principals pay attention to

---

* Portions of this chapter have been adapted from Fullan (1988) and Fullan (1991).

particular innovations, there will be a greater degree of implementation in the classrooms of the school. But there are two problems with this conclusion. First, despite a great deal of attention to the implementation role of principals during the 1980s, principals as dynamic change agents are still empirically rare – probably fewer than one in ten. Is this simply a function of training, selection, and support on the job, not yet catching up with practice? Or do we have the wrong conception of what the role should be?

Second, a great deal of the research, such as the findings on which we are basing new policies and expectations, is seriously limited in that it reports on what happens only to 'single' innovations. What a principal does with one innovation does not necessarily predict what he or she will do with another one. In a study of what influences principals' behaviour, Trider and Leithwood (1988) found that the content background of principals (naturally enough) influenced how much attention and effort they put into particular policies. For example, a background in special education would predict the amount of attention given to new special education policies, but not necessarily to that given to a new science priority. We just cannot generalize from studies of single innovations. Related, and more fundamentally, the reality is that principals are not contending with individual innovations or even a series of innovations. They are in the business of attempting to manage multiple innovations. Until we have many more studies which examine holistically the inside-out picture of how the principal does and could manage the 'field' of innovative possibilities facing him or her, we will be restricted in the conclusions we can draw.

Some of the more recent studies attempt to go beyond the problem of focusing on single innovations. Hall and Hord (1987) describe three types of principals: initiators, managers and responders, Initiators, for example, 'have clear, decisive long-range policies and goals that transcend, but include implementation of the current innovation'. However, the empirical base of their study of principals involves principals' behaviour in relation to single innovations. We do not know how these initiator principals deal with multiple innovations. Nor, to the extent that initiators are more effective, do we know how to develop more initiator principals compared to managers or responders.

Research on effective schools corroborates the findings of Hall and his colleagues and has proven rather conclusively that the principal is crucial to success. In a careful study of school effectiveness, Teddlie *et al.* (1989) paired eight schools in Louisiana in terms of consistent superior or inferior academic performance over a two-year period, matching the schools according to socio-economic status of the community. They found that the paired schools differed significantly in nine out of ten measures of teaching effectiveness drawn from the research literature (time on task, presentation of new material, high expectations, positive reinforcements, discipline, etc.). They identify differences in the role of the principal as a critical variable. In one of the pairs of schools that were identical (both had 50 per cent white and 50 per cent black students and were a few blocks from each other):

The principal at school 1 (the effective school) was described by one observer as 'having her finger on the pulse of the school'. She was frequently seen in the hallways and the classrooms; she was observed in her not infrequent role of teaching a class. She appeared knowledgeable regarding every significant innovation in every classroom and saw to it that teachers were exposed to new and creative ideas.

(Teddlie *et al.* 1989: 231)

By contrast

The principal at school 2 (the ineffective school) has had a teaching career marked with honors. This principal . . . stated that she had excellent dedicated teachers. Although never observed in the classroom, she was visible in the hallways. She welcomed visitors, conveying a 'nothing-to-hide' attitude . . . she praised her school and staff, saying that everything was 'just great'. 'Everything was just great', noted one observer, 'until we went into the classrooms'.

(Teddlie *et al.* 1989: 232)

Similarly, in their careful longitudinal study of fifty schools, Mortimore and associates (1988) single out 'purposeful leadership of the staff by the head-teacher' as key in schools found to be effective on a variety of academic and non-academic criteria. They describe some of the subtlety in what these effective heads did.

Purposeful leadership occurred where the headteacher understood the needs of the school and was involved actively in the school's work, without exerting total control over the rest of the staff. In effective schools, headteachers were involved in curriculum discussions and influenced the content of guidelines drawn up within the school, without taking complete control. They also influenced the teaching strategies of teachers, but only selectively, where they judged it necessary. This leadership was demonstrated by an emphasis on the monitoring of pupil's progress, through teachers keeping individual records. Approaches varied – some schools kept written records; others passed on folders of pupil's work to their next teacher; some did both – but a systematic policy of record keeping was important. With regard to in-service training, those heads exhibiting purposeful leadership did not allow teachers total freedom to attend any course; attendance was encouraged for a good reason.

(Mortimore *et al.* 1988: 250–1)

New conceptions of the principal

We have begun to make the transition from the principal's role in influencing the implementation of specific innovations to the principal's role in leading changes in 'the school as an organization'. The implication is that we have to look deeper and more holistically at the principal and the school as an organization. Louis and Miles (1990) make the distinction between *leadership* and *management* and emphasize that both are essential. Leadership relates to mission, direction, inspiration. Management involves designing and carrying out plans, getting things done, working effectively with people.

Louis and Miles list the main 'action motifs' for 'leadership' and 'management' for change. The leadership aspect involve articulating a vision, getting shared ownership, and evolutionary planning. The management function concerns negotiating demands and resource issues with the environment, and co-ordinated and persistent problem-coping (Louis and Miles 1990: ch. 2). Louis and Miles claim that management for change has been underestimated, must be conceived more broadly, and requires skills and abilities just as sophisticated as those for leadership. The main point is that both sets of characteristics are essential and must be blended or otherwise attended to within the same person or team.

The understanding of the principalship has been further advanced by the programmatic work of Leithwood and his colleagues. In earlier work they developed the 'principal's profile' which contained four levels of effectiveness (Leithwood and Montgomery 1986). The highest level was 'the problem-solver'. In their most recent work Leithwood and others have been attempting to unravel the meaning of problem solving by examining how 'expert' vs 'typical' principals go about solving actual problems.

Leithwood and Steinbach (1989a; 1989b) found that experts differed:

1 in the extent to which they explicitly took into account the interpretation others (teachers, for example) had of the problem
2 in viewing the problem in the context of the larger mission and problems in the school
3 in the degree of clarity they had about the problem and their ability to describe both their interpretation and the reasons they had for such interpretation.

They also found differences in how experts thought about goals (getting agreement with staff), values (being more cognizant and explicit about values), constraints (anticipating and identifying deeper problems), solution processes (using collaborative problem solving), and affect (not letting frustration get to them). Leithwood and Steinbach suggest that the principals' impact may be felt through their actions

   1 in generating better solutions to school problems
   2 in developing teachers' commitment to implementing such solutions
   3 in fostering long-term staff development.
                (Leithwood and Steinbach 1989a: 27)

In further work, Leithwood and Janzti (1990) compared principals who were particularly effective at transforming the culture of the school toward a stronger improvement orientation, with those principals who were less effective at school improvement. They found that the successful principals used six broad strategies. They took actions that

1 strengthened the school's [improvement] culture
2 used a variety of bureaucratic mechanisms to stimulate and reinforce cultural change
3 fostered staff development
4 engaged in direct and frequent communication about cultural norms, values and belief
5 shared power and responsibility with others
6 used symbols to express cultural values.

(Leithwood and Janzti 1990: 22)

We are beginning to obtain a more complex but clearer appreciation of the effective principal as a collaborative leader of continuous improvements in the school as an organization. Rosenholtz's (1989) study of 'stuck' and 'moving' schools is central to this new conception. Rosenholtz found that some schools in her sample were highly collaborative and effective for both teachers and students, while others were marked by mutual isolation and ineffectiveness. Her findings identify the importance of the principal in working with teachers to shape the school as a workplace in relation to shared goals, teacher collaboration, teacher learning opportunities, teacher certainty, teacher commitment, and student learning. To take but one example, Rosenholtz found that in collaborative settings 87 per cent of the teachers answered 'yes' to the question that asked whether their principal was a good problem-solver, compared with about 30 per cent in moderately or low-collaborative schools (1989: 55). Rosenholtz concludes:

> Great principals do not pluck their acumen and resourcefulness straight out of the air. In our data, successful schools weren't led by philosopher kings with supreme character and unerring method, but by a steady accumulation of common wisdom and hope distilled from vibrant, shared experience both with teacher leaders in schools and colleagues district wide.
>
> (Rosenholtz 1989: 219)

The role of the principal is not in implementing innovations or even in instructional leadership for specific classrooms. There is a limit to how much time principals can spend in individual classrooms. The larger goal is in transforming the culture of the school. If successful, it is likely that some advanced models of the future will show collaborative groups of teachers organizing and conducting learning, perhaps without the presence of a principal as we now know the role. The principal as the collaborative leader is the key to this future.

Action implications

Education changes of various sorts are constantly before the principal as reformers or reactors try to right the educational system. Whether a particular change is seen as a backward or forward step depends on our point of view, but all reforms are proposals for change. The principal is constantly being admonished to ensure or support implementation of this or that new policy or project. In Canada, revised provincial curriculum guidelines are always on the doorstep as the cyclical revision process continues *ad infinitum*. Legislation for special education, community-based programmes, and school-work options are added to the list along with any other project deemed important by school trustees or central district administrators. In the United States, it is all the more chaotic because more levels are involved. In addition to the local and state demands, the federal government, unlike in Canada, has had a strong indirect presence in local innovation. Categorical grants, federal legislation, Supreme Court rulings, and voluntary projects on every conceivable topic are being perpetrated on the educational system. It would not be unusual for a school district to be participating in fifty or more state or federally sponsored programmes at any one time, all of which have implications for the principal.

Every principal has a conception of his or her role; these conceptions vary, as we have seen, in that some principals are actively engaged in leading or facilitating change, while others are not. Certainly, different systems (school districts, states provinces) limit or facilitate change in different ways, but the starting-point from the individual principal's point of view should be a reflection on whether his or her own *conception* of the role of the principal has built-in limitations regarding change.

Principals within the same system operating in almost identical circumstances will work with change or avoid it, depending on *their* conception of the role. Just as teachers' sense of efficacy is important in bringing about school improvement, so is the principal's – perhaps more significant, because it affects *the whole organization*. We could also speculate that many principals are diffident about their change leadership role because they do not feel prepared or clear about how to carry it out.

What to do? The implementation perspective stresses that the starting-point for improvement is not system change, not change in others around us, but change in ourselves. A bias for action, focusing on short-term and long-term improvement, characterizes this perspective. The principal – all the more so, since he or she is in a critical leadership position – must take action and help create the conditions for others to take action. In a previous publication I offered ten guidelines for the individual principal formulated to contribute actions not words, and to overcome system inertia (Fullan 1988). It is essential that these guidelines be viewed in concert, not as actions isolated from one another.

1 Avoid 'if only' statements, externalizing the blame
2 Start small, think big: don't overplan or overmanage
3 Focus on something important like curriculum and instruction
4 Focus on something fundamental like the professional culture of the school
5 Practise fearlessness and other forms of risk-taking
6 Empower others below you
7 Build a vision relevant to both goals and change processes

8 Decide what you are *not* going to do
9 Build allies
10 Know when to be cautious.

Avoid 'if only' statements, externalizing the blame

In most cases, 'if only' statements beg the question, externalize the blame, and immobilize people. 'If only the superintendents were better leaders', 'if only the board would allocate more resources to professional development', 'if only the Ministry of Education would stop issuing so many policy changes', and so forth. All of these wishes for changes around us, according to Block (1987), are expressions of dependency and foster a sense of helplessness. As Block (1987: 16) sums it up, 'waiting for clear instructions before acting is the opposite of the entrepreneurial spirit'. Another way of putting it is, 'What can I do that is important to me and those around me?' The first guideline, then stresses the necessity for moving concretely in the direction of autonomy.

Start small, think big: don't overplan or overmanage

Complex changes (and managing multiple innovations in schools does represent complexity) means facing a paradox. On the one hand, the greater the complexity, the greater the need to address implementation planning; on the other hand, the greater the thoroughness of implementation planning, the more complex the change process becomes. The third and fourth guidelines describe what to focus on and the seventh guideline focuses on the need for a vision of the change process, but at this point, it seems necessary to caution against overplanning and overmanaging. As strategic and site-based planning models become more prevalent, we should shift our concern to worrying about the problem of 'implementing the implementation plan'. After a certain amount of goal and priority setting, it is important not to get bogged down in elaborate needs assessment, discussion of goals and the like. Striving for complexity in the absence of action can generate more clutter than clarity. Effective managers have the capacity to short circuit potentially endless discussion and wheel-spinning by getting to the action.

Recent evidence in both business and education indicates that effective leaders have an overall sense of direction, and start into action as soon as possible establishing small-scale examples, adapting, refining, improving quality, expanding, and reshaping as the process unfolds. This strategy might be summed up as start small; think big: or the way to get better at implementation planning is more by doing than by planning. Ownership is something that is developed through the process rather than in advance. Opportunities for reflection and problem-solving are more important during the process than before it begins. In this sense, innovations are not things 'to be implemented', but are catalysts, points of departure or vehicles for examining the school and for making improvements.

For complex changes, tighter forms of planning and managing lose on two counts. They place the principal in a dependent role, however unintended, and they hamper the extension of autonomy to teachers. Shared control over implementation at the school level is essential.

Focus on something important like curriculum and instruction

Here we become involved in setting priorities and questions of consistency as in the seventh guideline. Priorities are generated through a mixture of political and educational merit. The result, as we have seen, is overload. The best way for a principal to approach situations of impossible overload is to take the stance that 'we are going to implement a few things especially well, and implement other priorities as well as we would have anyway which is to keep them from getting out of hand'. Thus this is not a call for any new neglect. This guideline assumes that within the array of policy priorities, there are 'some things' which can productively be examined and improved. It takes policies not as all things to be implemented, but as some things to be exploited. What's worth fighting for is to select one area or a few instructional areas of major interest and/or need, and intensely purse them through implementation. For example, a serious attack on an important curriculum area for the school represents a strike for something that is close to the core educational goals of schools even if all potential priorities are not being addressed. Such a positive initiative can be pointed to as an example of commitment and accomplishment in spite of the overload that surrounds schools.

Moreover, there is much greater choice in what can be done than is normally acknowledged. In terms of ends, there are many policy priorities from which one can chose to emphasize. Within selected priority directions, the means of implementation can vary widely. For most policies it is more accurate to treat policy implementation as an opportunity to define and develop the policy further, than it is to conceive of it as putting into practice someone else's ideas. Principals, in effect, have enormous leeway in practice.

Consistency provides sustenance for setting priorities. The combination of overload and frequent, seeming shifts in policy results in a *de facto* eclecticism. Consistency in schools must be obtained at the receiving end not the delivery end. Local and provincial politics are the bane of sustained follow-through. Learning accrues in a school whose staff have 'a constructed, continuous shared reality'. Learning power comes from the consistent messages that students get about what it is to be an independent learner, a problem solver, a reader, a writer, and so forth. Conversely, schools that are eclectic in their approaches to learning (and the 'system' makes it easy to be eclectic) do poorly in terms of independent learning behaviours and achievement.

Focus on something fundamental like the professional culture of the school

In addition to concrete curriculum projects, the principal must pay attention to the professional culture of the school. The general notion is the evolution of a school, where, by virtue of being on the staff, teachers would actually become better at their work.

We know that professional cultures – with their openness to new ideas, the giving and the receiving of help, collegiality focused on instructional improvement – are strongly related to success of implementation. It is possible to work on professional cultures directly, but doing it through curriculum projects, as in the third guideline, is more effective. Thus curriculum projects would have a dual goal: first, to implement the curriculum, and second, to improve the interactive professionalism of teachers who participate in the project. To state it in another way, professional interactionism is both a strategy and an outcome. Fostering coaching and other forms of ongoing inservice should form a central part of any principal's priorities. When all is said and done in relation to a given project, one of the outcomes should be a greater sense of critical collegiality and professionalism among teachers. Each project, in other words, should increase the skill and willingness of teachers to work together on school improvements. Empowerment and vision building (sixth and seventh guidelines) are closely related to developing professional cultures of schools.

Practise fearlessness and other forms of risk-taking

Sarason (1971) described how some principals were carrying out certain practices at the same time that other principals in the same system were saying it was not allowed. How do they get away with it? It is somewhat superficial to say, but none the less true, that 'they just do it'.

Block (1987: 178ff) claims that many people take 'safe paths' in complex situations, such as believing simply in rationality, imitating others, or following the rules. He puts forward the idea that improvements are made through 'facing organizational realities' by 'continual acts of courage'. He suggests that if one is guided by vision building three 'acts' are necessary: 'facing the harsh reality', examining 'our own contribution to the problem', and making 'authentic statements in the face of disapproval'.

The tough version of acts of courage entails acting on something important, in such a way that we are 'almost indifferent to the consequences it might have for us' (Block 1987: 182). Like most risk-taking, we have to be prepared to lose before we can win. Paradoxically, effective principals, as the research literature indicates, are men and women who take independent stances on matters of importance, and in most cases are all the more respected for it. At a less dramatic level, I would suggest that fearlessness can be practised on a more modest scale. One need not start by publicly defying the director! Three criteria for beginning might be to be selective, to do it on a small scale, and to make a positive rather than a negative act of courage. So, for example, one might make it clear that the latest curriculum directive cannot be immediately addressed because the staff are in the midst of implementing another important priority. Then the principal can demonstrate willingness to discuss the importance and progress of this other priority. Another example might be presenting a well-worked-out plan, asking for modest resources to implement something important to the school and the community.

Empower others below you

As a safeguard against being wrong and because it is essential for implementing serious improvements in any case, empowering others in the school has to form a major component of the effective principal's agenda. It is becoming clearer in the research literature that complex changes in education may require active (top-down or external) initiation, but if they are to go anywhere, there must be a good deal of shared control and decision making during implementation.

From their current research Louis and Miles (1990) and others analyse the successful evolution of effective secondary school programmes. In addition to several other factors, many of which are related to the items on our list, Louis and Miles stress that while initiative often comes from the principal, 'power sharing' is critical from that point onward. Successful schools were characterized by principals who supported and stimulated initiative-taking by others, who set up cross-hierarchical steering groups consisting of teachers, administrators, and sometimes parents and students, and who delegated authority and resources to the steering group, while maintaining active involvement in or liaison with the groups.

As Patterson and his colleagues (1986) state, people become empowered when they can count on the support of the 'boss', can make or influence decisions affecting them and have access to information and resources enabling them to implement decisions. Patterson *et al.* (1986: 75–6) discuss the dilemma of leadership versus delegation. Too much freedom often results in a vague sense of direction and wasted time; clearly defined structure, on the other hand, often generates resistance or mechanical acceptance. In a statement that applies both to the relationship of school systems to schools, as well as principal to teachers, Patterson and colleagues state:

> Senior officials must strike a balance between giving up total control of the group and holding too tightly to the reins. Delegation, in its optimal sense, means initially setting the parameters, then staying involved through coordinating resources, reviewing progress reports, and being able to meet teams at critical junctures.
>
> (Patterson *et al.* 1986: 76)

Empowerment also means additional resources, such as time, money and personnel. Principals operating from an implementation perspective are especially adept at acquiring needed resources (Rosenholtz 1989; Smith and Andrews 1989; Louis and Miles 1990).

Build a vision relevant to both goals and change processes

Vision building feeds into and is fed by all other guidelines in this section. It cuts through the tendency to blame others; it provides a sense of direction for starting small but thinking big; it provides focus; it checks random fearlessness; it gives content to empowerment and alliance discussions; it gives direction for deciding what not to do. Above all, it permeates the enterprise with values, purpose and integrity for both the what and the how of improvement.

The vital role of vision appears in every book on educational and organizational excellence. It is not an easy concept with which to work, largely because its formation, implementation and shaping in specific organizations is a constant process. An organization, to be effective, needs both a vision of the nature or content that it represents, and a clear vision of the processes it characteristically values and follows.

Vision is not something that someone happens to have; it is a much more fluid process and does not have to be – indeed it must not be – confined to a privileged few. In a real sense, implementation of any policy will be superficial unless all implementers come to have a deeply held version of the meaning and the importance of the change for them.

To start with the leader, Bennis and Nanus (1985) make it quite clear that top leaders in their study had, but did not invent, visions for their organizations. Indeed, these leaders were more likely to be good at extracting and synthesizing images from a variety of sources:

> All of the leaders to whom we spoke seemed to have been masters at selecting, synthesizing, and articulating an appropriate vision of the future . . . If there is a spark of genius in the leadership function at all, it must lie in this transcending ability, a kind of magic, to assemble – out of all the variety of images, signals, forecasts and alternatives – a clearly articulated vision of the future that is at once single, easily understood, clearly desirable, and energizing.
>
> (Bennis and Nanus 1985: 101)

We normally think of vision as something in the future, but we do not necessarily think in terms of how to get to that vision When we do address the how, it is often formulated in a top-down manner: form a task force, clarify the vision, communicate and train it, assess it, etc. As we now turn more directly to the aspects of process, a number of the dimensions must be introduced. Working on one's own vision is the starting-point. The extension of this position is that it is the task of each person of the organization, to a certain extent, to create their own version of the vision of the future. But in working together visions will tend to converge, if the guidelines in this section are followed. This will sometimes result in sharper differences but the more serious problem seems to be the absence of clearly articulated visions, not a multiplicity of them.

It cannot be overemphasized that this guideline incorporates commitment to both the *content* of vision and to the *process* of vision building and implementation. It is in fact a dynamic and fluid relationship in which the vision of the school is shaped and reshaped as people try to bring about improvements. It is a difficult balance but commitment and skill in the change process on the part of organizational leaders and members is every bit as crucial as ideas about where the school should be heading.

The continuous process of vision building in an organization requires a number of skills and qualities. Two-way communication skills, risk-taking, the balancing of clarity and openness, the combining of pressure and support, integrity, positive regard for others, and a perpetual learning orientation, all figure in the dynamic process of developing a shared vision in the school. In Louis and Miles' (1990) terms, the process involves issues of *will* (such as risk-taking and tolerance of uncertainty) and *skill* (such as organizational design, the support of others, clear communication, the development of ownership). The shared vision, in short, is about the content of the school as it might become, and the nature of the change process that will get us there.

Decide what you are not going to do

If the principal tries to do everything that is expected, he or she expends incredible energy with little or nothing to show for it. Therefore, principals must learn how to say no selectively.

There are two features of principals' work which present them with aggravation. One is the endless stream of meetings and new policy and programme directives, already described. The other is a daily schedule which consists of continual interruptions. There are plenty of studies of the individual work-days of principals, and they draw the same conclusions: principals' work-days are characterized by dozens of small interactions. The research literature has come to label the work of principals as involving brevity, variety and fragmentation (Peterson 1985).

Principals, above all, are 'victims of the moment'. Because of the immediacy and physical presence of interruptions, principals are constantly dragged into the crises of the moment. These include telephone calls, two students fighting, salespeople, parents wanting to see them, calls from central office to check into something or to come to an urgent meeting, and so on. Dependency on the moment is not inevitable, however. Four strategies for maintaining initiative and control are: maintaining focus, making your position clear to the superintendent, managing time accordingly, and saying 'No'.

Vision building is central to selecting and maintaining focus. To simplify the matter, two issues are of first order importance; instructional leadership and public relations. Instructional leadership means working with teachers and others to decide on the most important needs of the school, whether it be English as a Second Language, language and writing across the curriculum, primary/junior science, or whatever. Responsiveness to the community is part and parcel of needs assessment and maintaining focus. Consent, and in some cases, involvement of parents, is essential. The priority in relation to the community is instructionally focused public relations, not random communication.

Making one's position clear to the first-line superintendent (area education officer) is ideally an interactive process. The emphasis should be on the principal taking charge. The principal, in effect, is saying to the superintendent that instructional leadership is his or her number one priority. The particular priorities arrived at may be done in full co-operation with the superintendent or in a more distant manner; in either case, the principal makes it a point that the superintendent understands the priority and the flow of actions being taken. The basic message is that if there is an important instructional activity in his or her school and there is a meeting which conflicts, he or she cannot attend the meeting but will send someone else. This is not a matter of being stubborn or rigid. Without such protection, a principal's time would get totally eaten up by unconnected activities which amount to nothing. By explaining one's position in terms of specific instructional activities, it turns out that very few meetings are so important that they cannot be missed. Many superintendents would value such a focus and stance, but let me say some would not. This is where selective fearlessness comes in. A little assertiveness in the service of a good cause where you have teacher and community backing may be necessary. There is nothing wrong with saying no. And we know that effective schools are characterized by a two-way communication and negotiation between principals and district superintendents (Coleman and La Rocque 1990).

Managing time is related to both attitude and technique. Protecting priority time, sometimes fiercely, is a must. Staying focused might mean, for example, setting aside a morning to plan a professional growth session for staff, and then sticking to it. It can be made clear that 'nobody is to interrupt' during that time. Exceptions may occur in extreme situations, but telephone calls, even aggressive ones, can be handled by a secretary, delayed or scheduled in.

Delegation, the third aspect of time management, is an orientation and skill that only a minority of middle managers have mastered. It amounts to the advice to try not to do anything that someone else in the building can do, because principals need to spend their time on what others in the building are not in a position to do. For example, why should a principal plan track and field days when teachers can do it better because it is for their students? Why should a principal collect and count trip money? Why should a principal fill out straightforward statistical reports, do the paperwork for teacher absence, and the like? The principal's job is to ensure that essential things get done, not to do them all himself or herself.

Saying 'No' is a summation of the advice of this guideline. Principals spend too much time on things that are not essential. There are few things that absolutely must be done, cannot be delayed or cannot be delegated. Only a small proportion of what principals do is centrally related to instruction apparently. Diversions, of course, also plague principals who have an instructional focus. But, they have learned to say no. Otherwise, the whole day would be spent running around with nothing to show for the effort except stress and with no sense of accomplishment other than short-term survival. Principals must get more in the habit of saying no, or of rescheduling things for a time when they can be addressed more efficiently.

Build allies

It is foolhardy to continue to act fearlessly if you are not at the same time developing alliances. One of the most encouraging developments since the mid-1980s is the presence of more and more potential allies who seem to want to support and move in the direction of greater school-based implementation (see Chapter 3). Criteria for promotion tend more and more to emphasize curricular leadership, capacity for working effectively with others and ability to lead interactive forms of development whether they involve coaching, performance appraisal or curriculum implementation.

With this potential, the principal should seek alliances, through specific projects and activities, with at least five groups: senior level administrators, peers, parents, subordinates, and individuals who are external to the system (in the Ministry of Education, Faculties of Education and so forth). As Patterson *et al.* (1986: 81) note, senior-level administrators are obviously crucial sources of power as sponsors and as responders to critical requests.

Peers – other principals and vice-principals – can also be significant sources of support in the short and long run. It may require some initiative and risk-taking, but principals who go out of their way to work co-operatively with other principals on a curriculum project and who share information and resources, develop both a reputation and a set of relationships which serve them well at points of critical decision.

Alliances with parents are much more tricky. One runs the risk of getting involved with splinter groups and/or offending important political forces on the board. Sticking with valued curriculum priorities can be one safeguard, because work with the community is intended not to block something, but to implement something considered to be valuable.

The sixth guideline stressed empowerment of teachers. Such empowerment is reciprocal. Teachers, for example, already have and exercise power *not* to do things. Building a trusted, empowered relationship with teachers usually means that the principal can count on teachers to help implement policies that the principal holds to be important, and vice versa. The empowerment pie becomes larger.

There are, of course, skills involved in negotiating relationships across the groups just described. Block (1987) talks about the critical skills of negotiating agreement and trust. He complicates the matter, realistically, by noting that such negotiations must be undertaken with both allies and adversaries. He outlines a number of steps for dealing with each of the following situations: high agreement/high trust (allies), high trust/low agreement (opponents), high agreement/low trust (bedfellows), low trust/unknown agreement (fence sitters), and low agreement/low trust (adversaries).

Know when to be cautious

Since people exert so much caution naturally, this section can be brief. Block mentioned four circumstances which dictate caution: when we don't know the situation, when survival is at stake, following periods of risk and expansion, and when we are in a zero trust environment (Block 1987: 17–18). Risks can also be reduced by starting small (and thinking big), trying out ideas on a small scale initially and/or with smaller numbers of people. However, if we are experiencing states of continuous, ever-increasing caution, that is a sign that either we ourselves should change or move elsewhere to a less repressive organization.

Conclusion

These guidelines thus do not assume that principals should passively implement system policies. On the contrary, we know enough about how changes get generated to know that the system is overloaded, and not all that coherent or co-ordinated (see Patterson *et al.* 1986). The school is the centre of change, and that is where focus, coherence, and consistency must be forged. And that is why the principal is so central to successful school improvement and reform.

The message for principals is that they should critically reflect on whether their own conceptions of the role are placing unnecessary limits on what can be done. This kind of reflection is difficult to undertake unaided, so that collaboration and feedback from teachers and other principals is needed. In assessing the need for change, principals should talk with teachers about their views. Knowledge and conceptions of the implementation perspective is a necessary foundation, to which must be added some knowledge or familiarity with the content of change and communication and interpersonal skills.

It may take some time to overcome teachers' historical experiences with principals, but the evidence shows that many teachers want to interact with colleagues on improvements and want direct support from principals. The principal is the key to creating the conditions for the continuous professional development of teachers and thus, of classroom and school improvement.

The burden on the principal is considerable, as Barth (1990) observes:

> If the teacher–principal relationship can be characterized as helpful, supportive, trusting, revealing of craft knowledge, so too will others. To the extent that teacher–principal interactions are suspicious, guarded, distant, adversarial, acrimonious, or judgmental, we are likely to see these traits pervade the school. The relationship between teacher and principal seems to have an extraordinary amplifying effect. It models what *all* relationships will be.
>
> (Barth 1990: 19, original emphasis)

In short, the school principal more than anyone else can bring successful school improvement into sharp focus.

5 Staff Development, Innovations and Institutional Development*

It is instructive to turn the implementation lens on staff development itself.† It has been well known for at least fifteen years that staff development and successful innovation or improvement are intimately related. However, even in the narrow sense of successful implementation of a single innovation, people have underestimated what it takes to accomplish this close interrelationship more fundamentally. I argue later in this chapter that we must go beyond the narrow conception of staff development to consider how it relates to institutional development of schools.

Staff development is conceived broadly to include any activity or process intended to improve skills, attitudes, understandings, or performance in present or future roles (Little 1989; Sparks and Loucks-Horsley 1990). Despite the fact that we know a great deal about what effective staff development looks like, it is still not well practised. There are at least two major and often mutually reinforcing reasons for this. One is technical – it takes a great deal of wisdom, skill and persistence to design and carry out successful staff development activities. The other is political. Staff development is a big business, as much related to power, bureaucratic positioning and territoriality as it is to helping teachers and students (see Little 1989; Paris 1989; Pink 1989).

The problem of harnessing staff development is compounded by its increasingly sprawling prominence. It is correctly seen as the central strategy for improvement, but it is frequently separated artificially from the institutional and personal contexts in which it operates.

The purpose of this chapter is to use the implementation perspective in order to provide clarity concerning the different ways in which staff development and innovation are related. Putting staff development in an innovation perspective should help us in sorting out where and how to put our energies into

---

* Adapted from Fullan (1990)
† The terms 'staff development', 'professional development', 'in-service' and 'ongoing assistance' are used interchangeably in this chapter.

approaches that will have both specific and lasting effects. I examine three different perspectives. The first is 'staff development as a strategy for implementation', and the second is 'staff development as an innovation' in its own right. 'Staff development as institutional development' is the third and more fundamental perspective. I conclude by claiming that the first two perspectives are useful for certain limited purposes but that only the third approach promises to make continuous staff development and improvement a way of life in schools.

Staff development as a strategy for implementation

In an earlier review, we established beyond doubt that staff development and effective implementation of innovations were strongly interrelated (Fullan and Pomfret 1977). The logic and evidence were fairly straightforward. As noted in Chapter 1, effective implementation consists of alterations in curriculum materials, practices and behaviour, and beliefs and understandings by teachers *vis-à-vis* potentially worthwhile innovations (regardless of whether the innovations are locally or externally developed). Put more simply, successful change involves learning how to do something new. As such, the process of implementation is essentially a learning process. Thus when it is linked to specific innovations, staff development and implementation go hand in hand.

At the same time (1977), in gross terms we learned that staff development should be innovation-related, continuous during the course of implementation, and involve a variety of formal (e.g. workshops) and informal (e.g. teacher-exchange) components. We also confirmed that most innovation attempts did not incorporate these characteristics. There were two things we did not know. First, we needed to identify some of the subprocesses of staff development and implementation success experienced by teachers. Second, although we could demonstrate that staff development and classroom implementation were closely linked, there was little evidence that these in turn were related to student achievement.

Since the earlier review, we have obtained further confirmation and additional insights into the link between staff development and implementation. As we discussed in Chapter 2, in examining the relationship between staff development and the implementation of microcomputers, virtually all studies of successful change, identify ongoing professional development as critical. Huberman and Miles (1984) for example found that the amount and quality of assistance was essential for addressing early implementation problems and for providing the pressure and support necessary for obtaining new skills and change in beliefs and understanding, which typically took two or more years.

The link between staff development and school achievement was not systematically demonstrated until recently. Stallings (1989) provides a precise response to this question. In several settings using different designs, Stallings and her colleagues set out to improve teaching and student achievement relative to reading practices in secondary schools. Stallings identified research findings on effective reading practices (i.e. the innovation), as well as research on critical factors related to effective staff development. Relative to the latter, Stallings states that teachers are more likely to change their behaviour and continue to use new ideas under the following conditions:

1 they become aware of a need for improvement through their analysis of their own observation profile
2 they make a written commitment to try new ideas in their classroom the next day
3 they modify the workshop ideas to work in their classroom and school
4 they try the ideas and evaluate the effect
5 they observe in each other's classrooms and analyse their own data
6 they report their success or failure to their group
7 they discuss problems and solutions regarding individual students and/ or teaching subject matter
8 they need a wide variety of approaches; modelling, simulations, observations, critiquing video tapes, presenting at professional meetings
9 they learn in their own way continuity to set new goals for professional growth.

(Stallings 1989: 3–4)

The cornerstones of the model, according to Stallings, are

1 learn by doing: try, evaluate, modify, try again
2 link prior knowledge to new information
3 learn by reflecting and solving problems
4 learn in a supportive environment: share problems and successes.

(Stallings 1989: 4)

Over the years, Stallings was able to compare the effects of three different training designs: the question was, what would the effect be on secondary students' reading scores . . .

1 if only reading teachers were trained and their students tested?
2 if all language arts teachers and reading teachers in a school were trained – hence reaching all students – and all students are tested?
3 if all teachers in a district were trained . . . over a three-year period, what would be the effect on the school district's level of reading at the end of ninth grade?

(Stallings 1989: 1–2)

Without going into all the details, the first design involved forty-seven teachers in seven districts, along with a control group. Teachers in the treatment group, compared with the control group, changed their behaviour in the classroom and their students gained six months in reading scores over the control group. In the second design, all teachers in two schools were trained and compared with a control group of two schools. The differential gain in reading scores was eight months. In the third study, all teachers in the district were provided with the training, with no control group. Each group of ninth grade students across three years of testing steadily improved their reading scores.

These impressive results demonstrate the power of a carefully designed staff development strategy for implementing single innovations.

Joyce *et al.* (1989), in their recent work in Richmond County, Georgia, provide further confirmation of the link between staff development, implementation, and student outcomes. After eighteen months of intensive training and follow-up with teams of teachers focusing on models of teaching, Joyce and his colleagues were able to claim considerable (but variable) implementation in the classroom, which in turn was related to a dramatic impact on student achievement and student promotion rates.

It is worth emphasizing that both the Stallings and Joyce initiatives required considerable sophistication, effort, skill, and persistence to accomplish what they did. Most staff development activities do not measure up to these standards, as Pink's (1989) review of four change projects illustrates. He found twelve barriers to innovation effectiveness that were common to all four projects. Paraphrased, they are as follows:

  1 an inadequate theory of implementation, including too little time for teachers to plan for and learn new skills and practices
  2 district tendencies toward faddism and quick-fix solutions
  3 lack of sustained central office support and follow-through
  4 underfunding the project, or trying to do too much with too little support
  5 attempting to manage the projects from the central office instead of developing school leadership and capacity
  6 lack of technical assistance and other forms of intensive staff development
  7 lack of awareness of the limitations of teacher and school administrator knowledge about how to implement the project
  8 the turnover of teachers in each school
  9 too many competing demands or overload
  10 failure to address the incompatibility between project requirements and existing organizational policies and structures
  11 failure to understand and take into account site-specific differences among schools
  12 failure to clarify and negotiate the role relationships and partnerships involving the district and the local university, who in each case had a role, albeit unclarified, in the project.

(Pink 1989: 22–4)

In short, staff development, implementation of innovation, and student outcomes are closely interrelated, but because they require such a sophisticated, persistent effort to co-ordinate, they are unlikely to succeed in many situations. Any success that does occur is unlikely to be sustained beyond the tenure or energy of the main initiators of the project.

Staff development as an innovation

A second useful but still limiting perspective is to consider major new staff development projects as innovations in their own right. In particular, policies and structures that establish new roles, such as mentors, coaches and the like, are and can be considered as innovations in the states and districts in which they are adopted. The question is whether our knowledge about the dos and don'ts of introducing curriculum innovations is applicable to introducing new mentoring and coaching practices. This section provides some support for the notion that the establishment of new staff development roles or projects would benefit from knowledge of implementation theory.

In a recent review, Little (1990b) has applied such a perspective to the evolution of the mentoring phenomenon. As Little states: 'those who would implement mentor roles are confronted with a two-part challenge: to introduce classroom teachers to a role with which they are unfamiliar; and to introduce the role itself to an institution and occupation in which it has few precedents' (1990b: 7–8). In reviewing empirical studies, Little identified three implementation problems: the pace of implementation, lack of opportunity to carry out the role, and precedents that constrain mentors' performance.

It is well known that major policy initiatives are often introduced rapidly, with little thought or time given to consider implementation (Fullan 1991). Among other studies, Little cites California's Mentor Teacher programme:

> California launched a precipitous schedule of implementation . . . A schedule of implementation limited to the state's fiscal year propelled them toward quick decisions about the form it would assume. The result was a pervasive effort to bring the definition of the mentor role within the boundaries of familiar roles and functions. Based on nine case studies and a summary of 291 districts, Bird (1986) concludes that, 'a good deal was lost, and little or nothing gained, by haste in implementing the mentor program'.
>
> (Little 1990b: 9–10)

Rapid starts involving complex innovations often result in simplifying and reducing the intended scope of the change. Little notes Huberman and Miles's observation based on their twelve case studies of innovation:

> Smooth early use was a bad sign. Smoothly implementing sites seemed to get that way by reducing the initial scale of the project and by lowering the gradient of actual practice change. This 'downsizing' got rid of most headaches during the initial implementation but also threw away most of the potential rewards: the project often turned into a modest, sometimes trivial enterprise.
>
> (Huberman and Miles 1984: 273)

A second problematic area of implementation relates to selection criteria, pre–implementation training for mentors, and support during implementation, which Little sums up under the general label of 'opportunity'. She starts with selection criteria, indicating the importance of basing selection of mentors on their expertise and credibility – both as classroom teachers and as colleagues who had track records of working successfully with other teachers. Little also found that pre-implementation training for mentors was variable, often focusing only on general process skills. Relative to post-selection support, Bird and Alspaugh (1986) found that 40 per cent of districts participating in the first two years of California's mentor programme allocated no resources to support mentors during implementation.

Coaching faces similar implementation problems, but not on the same scale because, unlike mentoring, coaching projects have tended to be less formal (e.g. not involving legislation or formal policy), more voluntary, and smaller in scale. Coaching projects, perhaps because of these characteristics, have proliferated at a rapid rate. Many so-called coaching projects, as we shall discuss in the next section, appear to be superficial. Even if we assume rigorous coaching designs, the innovation perspective is instructive.

We can take as an example Joyce and Showers's (1988) work because it is more developed and available in the literature. According to Joyce and Showers, coaching programmes represent powerful strategies for implementing instructional improvements that impact on student learning. In their work coaching is attached to training, continuous, experimental in nature, and separate from supervision and evaluation. It involves theory–demonstration–practice–feedback and follow-through support.

The innovation perspective is revealing because it starts with the question 'In what respects is coaching an innovation?' Joyce and Showers's work implies at least three types of innovations for school systems. First, it represents a change in the technology of training. Coaching leaders have to learn and carry out a sophisticated training programme over a period of time. Second, it involves organizing study groups of teachers at the school level. This entails restructuring the workplace in a more collegial mode. Third (and related but more fundamental than the previous point), coaching implicitly raises questions about the deeper collaborative work cultures of schools, and the role of teachers as professionals.

Joyce and Showers (1988) have effectively tackled the first problem. They are able to implement the training model with desired effects. They are in the midst of working on the second problem – organizing study groups in individual schools within a district (Joyce *et al.* 1989). The third problem – how to change the culture of the organization – remains unaddressed.

The implications of this analysis are quite profound. While most districts do not provide the training support, the problem is much deeper than that. Even if districts were to address the training and study group issues, coaching as an innovation would be short lived. It would be just another *ad hoc* innovation that has a short half-life. The danger is that coaching, which has powerful potential, will be trivialized, because the organizational necessities and cultural change implied by coaching will be missed altogether, or addressed superficially.

It should be obvious that I am not advocating that coaching or mentoring projects become innovations as ends in themselves. Many such projects, for example, do not appear to be focused or clear about their pedagogical and student learning objectives. Joyce and Showers (1988), contrary to popular belief, have never advocated coaching *per se*. Rather 'the major purpose of peer coaching programs is implementation of innovations to the extent that determination of effects on students is possible' (1988: 83). In pursuing this goal, I have suggested that it is important to consider coaching and mentoring as innovations, which they are, provided that one does not stop there.

Although mentoring and coaching have great potential, as long as they are treated as innovations or projects or even as strategies, their impact will be superficial and short-term and will be confined to a few participants. It is the ultimate thesis of this chapter that our attention must shift explicitly to how staff development fits into long-term institutional purposes and development of schools.

Staff development as institutional development

By institutional development, I mean changes in schools as institutions that increase their capacity and performance for continuous improvements. The domain is the culture of the school as a workplace (Sarason 1971; Little 1982; Rosenholtz 1989). I want to start by examining the relationship between the culture of the school and the two perspectives just considered. This will amount to a critique of the limitations of the two perspectives. Second, it will pave the way for describing what it means to focus directly and more systematically on institutional development. I will provide an example from our current work. Finally, three major implications for staff development will be outlined. As we push the implementation perspective deeper we inevitably confront the need to change institutions, not just to implement the latest favoured innovation.

To start with the 'strategy for implementation' perspective, teacher collegiality and other elements of collaborative work cultures are known to be related to the likelihood of implementation success (Fullan and Pomfret 1977, Little 1982). Thus all other things being equal, schools characterized by norms of collegiality and experimentation are much more likely to implement innovations successfully. The first point to be made is that those using staff development for implementation should take into account the nature of teacher collegiality that exists in the schools with which they intend to work. For example, as impressive as Stallings's (1989) staff development design is, there is no mention of these school level variables, which must have had effects that remain unknown on implementation and institutionalization. In other words, staff developers must work with schools as organizations as much as they work with individuals or small groups of teachers.

The second point to be noted is that even when teacher collegiality is taken into account, it is usually treated as a contextual factor or as a 'given', that is it is used to explain differences in implementation more or less along the lines that some schools happen to be more collegial than others.

Third, it can be argued, at least hypothetically, that solid staff development projects, like that of Stallings, in addition to having a positive impact on change in teacher practice and student achievement, can also have a spin-off or residual impact on increasing collegiality among teachers. Put another way, since good staff development practices always incorporate teacher–teacher sharing and interaction, they could, if successful, demonstrate the value of new norms of collegiality. At a minimum, it would seem that people using the staff development for implementation strategy should explicitly concentrate on the dual goals of implementing a project successfully and influencing the collegial climate of the school as an organization. This would be a useful contribution, but I am afraid that the culture of the school is much too strong to be influenced for any length of time (or at all in some cases) by single, passing projects – no matter how well designed.

The coaching and mentoring phenomenon is much more intriguing. On the surface, it looks like these strategies are indeed tantamount to attempting to change the collaborative culture of the school. In fact, they are not.

Coaching is particularly instructive for examining the underlying issues. There are at least three basic problems: the relationship of coaching to the culture of the school; the form and content of coaching; and the need for a more objective and balanced appreciation of the complex relationship between autonomy and collaboration. In effect, these three problem areas amount to cautioning advocates of coaching and collaboration against assuming that working toward increased interaction among teachers is automatically a good thing.

Coaching and the culture of the school

As we have seen, coaching, mentoring and other similar arrangements usually involve pairs or small groups of teachers working together. As such they represent only a small subpart of the total culture of the school. Thus, whether or not a particular coaching project finds itself in a hospitable environment (i.e. a school in which a collegial climate predated the coaching initiative) is a very important variable. Seller and Hannay (1988) examined a well-designed coaching project in two high schools and found that the pre-existing climate of collegiality explained whether or not the project was successful. At a minimum, the advice to those advocating coaching is to take into account the total culture of the school before deciding to proceed. One can also infer that even good coaching programmes do not alter the culture of the school. Although coaching can be intentionally designed as a strategy for increasing the collaborative work culture of the school, there is no evidence that this by itself will work. Normative cultures are not that easily influenced.

Form and content of coaching

Little (1990a) has provided the clearest exposition of the importance of considering variations in the form and content of collegiality. Form involves the degree and type of collaborative relationship. She suggests that there are at least four types of relationships ranked along an independence–interdependence continuum: storytelling and scanning for ideas, aid and assistance, mutual sharing, and joint work. In Little's words:

> The move from conditions of complete independence to thorough–going interdependence entails changes in the frequency and intensity of teachers' interactions, the prospects for conflict, and probability of influence. That is, with each successive shift, the warrant for autonomy shifts from individual to collective judgement and preference.
>
> (Little 1990a: 5)

Little claims that the first three forms – storytelling, assistance, and sharing – represent 'weak ties' of collegiality. Little (1990a) cites evidence that most coaching and mentoring projects are of this relatively superficial, safe, inconsequential variety, and hence have little impact on the culture of the school. For Little, it is joint work that has the greatest potential because it involves

> encounters among teachers that rest on shared responsibility for the work of teaching . . . collective conceptions of autonomy, support for teachers initiative and leadership with regard to professional practice, and group affiliations grounded in professional work. Joint work is dependent on the structural organization of task, time and other resources in ways not characteristic of other forms of collegiality.
>
> (Little 1990a: 14–15)

Little stresses that the content, not just the form of collaboration, is also critical.

> The content of teachers' values and beliefs cannot be taken for granted in the study or pursuit of teachers' collegial norms of interaction and interpretation. Under some circumstances, greater contact among teachers can be expected to advance the prospects for students' success; in others, to promote increased teacher-to-teacher contact may be to intensify norms unfavourable to children.
>
> (Little 1990a: 22)

Further, Little asks:

> Bluntly put, do we have in teachers' collaborative work the creative development of well informed choices, or the mutual reinforcement of poorly informed habit? Does teachers' time together advance the understanding and imagination they bring to their work, or do teachers merely confirm one another in present practice? What subject philosophy and subject pedagogy do teachers reflect as they work together, how explicit and accessible is their knowledge to one another? Are there collaborations that in fact erode teachers' moral commitments and intellectual merit?
>
> (Little 1990a: 22)

Autonomy and collaboration

We cannot assume that autonomy is bad and collaboration is good. One person's isolation is another person's autonomy; one person's collaboration is another person's conspiracy. Flinders (1988) speaks to the former:

> The teachers I observed not only accepted their relative isolation but actively strove to maintain it. At those points in the day when teachers had the greatest discretion over their use of time (during lunch breaks and preparation time), they typically went out of their way to avoid contact with others . . . Teachers used their classrooms as sanctuaries during breaks as well as before and after school, remaining alone in their rooms to prepare lessons instead of working in their department offices where collegial interaction would have been more available.
>
> (Flinders 1988: 23)

Flinders claims that for many teachers isolation is a strategy for getting work done because 'it protects time and energy required to meet immediate instructional demands' (1988: 25). Flinders observes that most of us seek periods of independent work in order to meet obligations:

> It is not uncommon to respond to increased job demands by closing the office door, canceling luncheon appointments, and 'hiding out' in whatever ways we can. We do not attribute our motives for such behaviour to naturally conservative personality traits or to malevolent or unprofessional regard for out colleagues. On the contrary, it is professional norms that dissuade us from sacrificing our commitments to job responsibilities even when such a sacrifice can be made in the name of collegiality.
>
> (Flinders 1988: 25)

None of this is to deny that isolation can be a protection from scrutiny and a barrier to improvement, but it does say that we must put the question of autonomy and collaboration in a perspective conducive to assessing the conditions under which each might be appropriate.

Hargreaves (1991) formulates a useful typology for considering school cultures. He suggests that there are four types: fragmented individualism, balkanization, contrived collegiality, and collaborative cultures. Fragmented individualism is the traditional form of teacher isolation so clearly depicted by Lortie (1975). Balkanization, often found in high schools, consists of subgroups and cliques operating as separate sub-entities, often in conflict with each other when major decisions have to be made.

> The designation contrived collegiality is new: [It] is characterized by a set of formal, specific bureaucratic procedures . . . It can be seen in initiatives such as peer coaching, mentor teaching, joint planning in specially provided rooms, formally scheduled meetings and clear job descriptions and training programs for those in consultative roles.
>
> (Hargreaves 1991: 19)

Contrived collegiality can ignore the real culture of the school and lead to a proliferation of unwanted contacts among teachers that consume already scarce time with little to show for it (see also Hargreaves 1989).

Hargreaves and Dawe (1989) elaborate on the problem of contrived collegiality by claiming that many forms of coaching are too technical, narrow, and short-term in focus. They argue that the current move away from teacher isolationism is locked into a struggle involving two very different forms of collegiality:

> In the one, it is a tool of teacher empowerment and professional enhancement, bringing colleagues and their expertise together to generate critical yet also practical-grounded reflection on what they do as a basis for wiser, more skilled action. In the other, the breakdown of teacher isolation is a mechanism designed to facilitate the smooth and uncritical adoption of preferred forms of action (new teaching styles) introduced and imposed by experts from elsewhere, in which teachers become technicians rather than professionals exercising discretionary judgment.
>
> (Hargreaves and Dawe 1989: 7)

Strong collaborative cultures, according to Hargreaves (1991), are deep, personal, and enduring. They are not 'mounted just for specific projects or events. They are not strings of one-shot deals. Cultures of collaboration rather are, constitutive of, absolutely central to, teachers' daily work' (Hargreaves 1991: 14).

In short, collegially oriented staff development initiatives either fail to address the more basic question of school culture, or vastly underestimate what it takes to change them. There is also evidence that collaborative cultures, when they do occur, are achieved through the extraordinary efforts of individuals. Often, such efforts either cannot be sustained over time or are vulnerable to the inevitable departure of key individuals (Hargreaves 1989; Little 1990a). In other words, what is at stake are basic changes in the professional institution of schooling.

An illustration

The main implication of this chapter is to refocus staff development so that it becomes part of an overall strategy for professional and institutional reform. We provide here one illustration taken from our current work in the Learning Consortium. Although we do not claim that it represents a full-blown example, it reflects movement toward the type of comprehensive conception and strategy required for substantial institutional development of schools. Space permits only a brief description of the framework (for more information see Fullan *et al.* 1990b; Watson and Fullan 1991).

The Learning Consortium is a three-year partnership among four major school districts and two higher education institutions in the greater Toronto area. There are two overriding assumptions in the consortium. One is to design

and carry out a variety of activities that make the professional and staff development continuum a reality (from the Bachelor of Education through pre-
service, induction, and career-long developments). The second major assump-
tion is that classroom and school improvement must be linked and integrated if
serious improvements are to be achieved.

We will not describe the various activities here, but they involve Summer
Institutes and follow-up, cadre staff development and support, leadership in-
service, team development in schools, and the like. They focus on instructional
improvements like the use of co-operative learning strategies, as well as on
school-wide changes involving greater collaboration.

Our goal is to understand and influence both classroom improvement and
school improvement through identifying and fostering systematic links between the two. The framework for analysis and action we are developing is
contained in Figure 5.1. For classroom improvement, we and others have
found that teachers must work simultaneously (but not necessarily at the same
pace) on all four sub-cogs. For both teachers and students, the combined
capacity to manage the classroom, the continuous acquisition of proven instructional strategies and skills, and the focus on desired educational goals and
content are essential.

The sub-cogs in the far right of Figure 5.1 relate to school improvement.
There is considerable evidence, we think, that the more basic features of school
improvement (as distinct from a list of effective schools characteristics) are the
following four. Schools improve when they have, or come to have, a shared

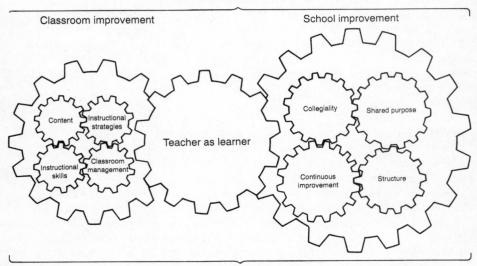

Figure 5.1 A comprehensive framework for classroom and school improvement
Source: Fullan, Bennett and Rolheiser-Bennett (1990)

purpose, norms of collegiality, norms of continuous improvement, and structures that represent the organizational conditions necessary for significant improvement (Little 1987; Rosenholtz 1989). Note that these are not individual characteristics. They are discrete and measurable features of collectivities – in this case, people in schools.

It is necessary to comment on the interrelationship of the school improvements cogs. Shared purpose includes such things as vision, mission, goals, objectives and unity of purpose. It refers to the shared sense of purposeful direction of the school relative to major educational goals. Shared purpose is of course not static, nor does it arise by itself. The other three cogs in interaction constantly generate and (re)shape purpose. Norms of collegiality refer to the extent to which mutual sharing, assistance and joint work among teachers is valued and honoured in the school. As stated earlier, there is nothing particularly virtuous about collaboration *per se*. It can serve to block change or put down students as well as to elevate learning. Thus collegiality must be linked to norms of continuous improvement and experimentation in which teachers are constantly seeking and assessing potentially better practices inside and outside their own school (and contributing to other people's practice through dissemination). And, as the framework depicts, commitment to improving student engagement and learning must be a pervasive value and concern.

We use structure in the sociological sense to include organizational arrangements, roles and formal policies that explicitly build-in working conditions that, so to speak, support and press for movement in the other cogs. Time for joint planning, joint teaching arrangements, staff development policies, new roles such as mentors, and school improvement procedures are examples of structural change at the school level that is conducive to improvement.

The centrepiece, or bridge, linking and overlapping classroom and school improvement in Figure 5.1 is the teacher as learner. There are two absolutely critical features of this component of the framework. First, we see four aspects of teacher as learner – technical, reflective, inquiry, and collaborative – which must be seen in combination. Each has its separate tradition of research and practice, and each has made important contributions in its own right. The mastery of technical skills increases instructional certainty; reflective practice enhances clarity, meaning and coherence; inquiry fosters investigation and exploration; collaboration enables one to receive and give ideas and assistance.

Although many approaches address aspects of all four features of the teacher as learner in one way or another, all models to this point have a central tendency to stress only one or two of the four. Rarely (and we would say never in a fundamental sense) have all four received intensive attention in the same setting. It is easier said than done. The question is how can the strengths of each of these four traditions be integrated and established in the teacher as learner.

The second critical feature is to distinguish between specific and generic levels of development of the teacher as learner. By specific I mean how particular improvements are experienced and designed. For example, one can start with a technical instructional innovation, such as co-operative learning, and find that it has consequences for all four aspects of the teacher as learner (which is in fact how we started). Similarly, one could begin with any of the other three sub-cogs – an action research project, for example – and proceed to incorporate the development of technical instructional skills, reflective methods, and so forth. We do not know enough yet about the very difficult conceptual and strategic questions of whether it is better to start with a single teacher-learner dimension (and if so, which one), or to work on all four equally.

A more fundamental point at this time is the recognition that teachers (remember that we are still talking about the teacher as individual learner) can come to develop the generic capacity to function on all four cylinders. In this case, it is not just being good at co-operative learning but mastering an array of instructional models; it is not just being involved in a reflective practice project but being a reflective practitioner; it is not participating on an action research investigation but conducting constant inquiry; it is not being part of a peer coaching project, but being collaborative as a way of working. In short, teachers come to internalize these ways of being to the point where it becomes second nature to be a perpetual learner.

Now it is precisely when every teacher in the school develops this 'generic capacity' to learn that classroom improvement and school improvement entirely overlap. Such an ideal will never be achieved of course, but one can immediately see how powerful the bridge can become when a school experiences a significant increase in the proportion of staff who are learners as we have defined the term.

Two final aspects of the framework revolve around the singularly important question of what drives the framework. It is, after all, not self-generating. One of two key driving factors is the presence of student engagement and learning as a pervasive preoccupation. We propose that the impact on all students be front and centre for every cog and interrelationship among the cogs. Constant valuing and attention to student engagement and learning can be a powerful motivating force, if it is integrated with movement in the cogs. The second agent of change is leadership and mobilization. We explicitly rejected the idea that leadership be a particular component of the framework. Leadership can, does, and must come from a variety of different sources in different situations (and different sources in the same situation over time). Leadership for success variously comes from the principal, key teachers, the superintendent, parents, trustees, curriculum consultants, governments, universities, and so on. As the list reveals, the driving force for change can initially come from inside or outside the school and from a variety of different roles. Once the model is fully functioning, leadership does indeed come from multiple sources simultaneously.

The Learning Consortium has been operating for a little more than two years. It has been successful in mobilizing a great number of people to action which they and others agree has resulted in improvements in classrooms and schools. We do not think that the Learning Consortium, as much as it is becoming integrated into the lives of the institutions involved, will end up deeply affecting collaborative work cultures in the sense that Hargreaves and

Little use the term. Nias *et al.*'s (1989) study illustrates how rich and complex collaborative cultures really are.

We do see very clearly, however, that the multi-level and multifaceted staff development activities that occur in all large school districts are, in the case of the Learning Consortium, being harnessed and interrelated in a more coherent and synergistic manner. There are still dilemmas between autonomy and collaboration, but staff development in these districts is becoming less fragmented and desultory, more purposeful, and more linked to classroom and school development as defined by teachers and principals.

Implications

Staff development will never have its intended impact as long as it is grafted on to schools in the form of discrete, unconnected projects. The closer one gets to the culture of schools and the professional lives of teachers, the more complex and daunting the reform agenda becomes. More powerful strategies are needed for more powerful changes. At least three strands of the problem require radical rethinking and integration, namely the individual, the school, and the district.

First, those involved in staff development must think and act more holistically about the personal and professional lives of teachers as individuals. As we have seen, many staff development projects provide temporary resources and incentives for particular changes (e.g. Stallings 1989) but do not amount to much in the bigger scheme of teachers' lives (Smylie 1988). Huberman's (1989) research clearly shows the importance of recognizing career and life cycle experiences of teachers. What is at stake is the reconceptualization of the professional role of teachers (Fullan *et al.* 1990a). Staff development in this view becomes the sum total of formal and informal learning experiences accumulated across one's career. The agenda then is to work continuously on the spirit and practice of lifelong learning for all teachers.

The second element involves working more organically with the school as an organization. This is turning out to be both complex and powerfully resistant to influence. It is not at all clear how autonomy and collaboration should be balanced. We do know, however, how powerful the school culture is. For example, despite massive effort and support over eighteen months, and despite some remarkable success in student achievement, Joyce *et al.* (1989: 15) comment on the fragility of their accomplishments: 'It depends on about forty teachers – only ten per cent of the total'.

We have seen that many of the reform efforts actually work at cross-purposes to intended directions by creating unnecessary status differences, role ambiguities, and superficial, inefficient relationships (Hargreaves and Dawe 1989; Smylie and Denny 1989; Little 1990a).

There are endemic difficulties to establishing and maintaining collaborative work cultures. Nias *et al.* (1989) found that teachers had great difficulty collaborating even when they wanted to work together. When collegiality is achieved, it is often short-lived because the social organization of the workplace is not conducive to maintaining collaboration in the long run (Smylie 1988; Little 1990a; Hargreaves 1991). Restructuring schools is complex and unclear (Elmore 1990) and will involve a long-term effort led by those within schools (Fullan 1988; Fullan and Hargreaves 1991). Finally, the centralization of policy-making and resources for staff development must be reconfigured. Little's (1989) examination of district policy for staff development in California reveals the problem. Central office administrators and staff development specialists designed and delivered over two-thirds of the staff development experienced by teachers across thirty districts. 'Leader time' was one of the highest cost items, more so than costs for time allocated to support learners (teacher participants). Many of the studies of mentoring reviewed by Little (1990b) also documented the centralization of staff development resources, which were devoted to supporting activities directed outside rather than inside schools. In the area of curriculum change, Paris (1989) chronicles the struggle between increased curriculum control at the district level and the uphill battle of one innovative school.

Neither centralization nor decentralization has worked in achieving educational reforms. The lines of development involving individuals, schools and districts will require close collaboration between those inside and outside schools. Pursuing the implementation perspective in this instance leads us to the conclusion that staff developers have a much bigger role to play in teacher development than hitherto realized. Successful school improvement as a continuous capacity will never be achieved in the absence of making staff development and institutional development an integrated reality.

6 Beyond Implementation: Teacher Development and Educational Reform*

The implementation perspective with its spotlight on practice and its disposition towards action and improvement pushes us deeper toward more basic problems and solutions. We have come to realize the futility of implementing one innovation at a time, even serious ones. Ten years ago we 'studied innovations'; today we are 'doing reform'. There has been a shift from passivity to action, and from narrowness to comprehensiveness of solutions. We may know more, but we are also taking on more.

In the course of this development, the concept implementation has revealed its own limitations. The very term connotes 'something to be put in practice'. It focuses on the object of change thereby detaching it in artificial ways from people and their ongoing circumstances. It has a bias implying that innovations are externally introduced. Beyond implementation alters the lens from innovations *per se* to the day-to-day actions of individuals in organizational settings. There has been a move from implementation to individual and institutional development. The latter is more basic – second-order change into today's jargon (Cuban 1988). In individual and institutional development, how people and organizations cope with the daily demands of maintenance and change becomes the anchor point. Beyond implementation leads us to consider more holistic, and organic questions of how individuals and organizations can become better equipped to manage multiple changes as normal fare. Here success is not whether a given innovation is implemented, but whether the basic capacity to deal with change has developed.

One of the pivotal questions in this new perspective beyond implementation is how the profession of teaching develops. I see two countervailing forces. One I have called 'intensification;' the other 'restructuring'. Relative to the former:

---

* Parts of this chapter are adapted from Fullan (1991).

Increased definition of curriculum, mandated textbooks, standardized tests tightly aligned with curriculum, specification of teaching and administrative methods backed up by evaluation, and monitoring all serve to intensify as exactly as possible the what and how of teaching.

(Fullan 1991: 16)

Restructuring takes many forms but it:

usually involves school-based management; enhanced roles for teachers in instruction and decision-making; integration of multiple innovations; restructured timetables supporting collaborative work cultures; radical reorganization of teacher education; new roles such as mentors, coaches, and other teacher leader arrangements; and revamping and developing the shared mission and goals of the school among teachers, administrators, the community and students.

(Fullan 1991: 16)

While restructuring is on the right track it is not without its problems. Changing structures is easier to bring about than changes in values, beliefs, behaviour and other normative and cultural changes. One of the core aspects of cultural change is how the profession of teaching evolves in this attempted new order. In this chapter I examine the relationships between the teacher education continuum and school development. I then consider the problem of sustaining improvement, even if we get started in the right direction. I conclude that teacher development and professionalism is at the crossroads, which means that the chances for reform are at the crossroads.

The teacher education continuum and school development

I make two key assumptions: first, teacher education is a matter of life-long learning, starting before one enters teacher pre-service (probationary period) and continuing throughout one's career (Fullan *et al.* 1990a); second, teacher development and school development must go hand in hand. You cannot have one without the other. These assumptions lead us to examine more closely teacher education programmes, and the working conditions of teachers, especially in relation to prospects for teacher development vs teacher stagnation or burnout.

Let us start at the beginning with initial teacher preparation. It is a very discouraging picture. Sarason and colleagues in 1962 wrote a book in which they called teacher preparation 'an unstudied problem'. They revised the book twenty-four years later observing:

The fundamental question we address in this book: what is the relationship between the preparation of teachers and the realities they experience when they embark on a career? That question is as unstudied today – as superficially discussed today – as in previous decades.

(Sarason *et al.* 1986: xiv)

Goodlad and his colleagues have just completed a large-scale research investigation in the United States called *A Study of the Education of Educators* (Goodlad 1990a; 1990b). They confirmed in detail what a lot of people knew and feared

– that teacher education policy and practice is in bad shape lacking coherence or simply wrong-headed. Goodlad (1990a) proposed four sets of expectations for teacher education programmes:

1 that they will prepare teachers to enculturate the young into a political democracy
2 that they will provide teachers with the necessary intellectual tools and subject-matter knowledge
3 that they will insure that teachers have a solid initial grounding in pedagogy
4 that they will develop in teachers the beginning levels of the knowledge and skills required to run our schools.

(Goodlad 1990a: 699)

They found that the programmes they studied fell far short of these expectations. Among their main findings:

1 The preparation programs in our sample made relatively little use of the peer socialization processes employed in some other fields of professional preparation. There were few efforts to organize incoming candidates into cohort groups or to do so at some later stage. Consequently, students' interactions about their experiences were confined for the most part to formal classes (where the teaching is heavily didactic). The social, intellectual, and professional isolation of teachers, so well described by Dan Lortie, begins in teacher education. This relatively isolated individualism in preparation seems ill-suited to developing the collegiality that will be demanded later in site-based school renewal.
2 The rapid expansion of higher education, together with unprecedented changes in academic life, have left professors confused over the mission of higher education and uncertain of their role in it. Although the effects of these changes in academic life transcend schools and departments, the decline of teaching in favor of research in most institutions of higher education has helped lower the status of teacher education. In regional public universities, once normal schools and teachers colleges, the situation has become so bad that covering up their historic focus on teacher education is virtually an institutional rite of passage. Teaching in the schools and teacher education seem unable to shake their condition of status deprivation.
3 There are serious disjunctures in teacher education programs: between the arts and sciences portion and that conducted in the school or department of education, from component to component of the so-called professional sequence, and between the campus-based portion and the school based portion . . . It is also clear from our data that the preparation under way in the programs we studied focused on *classrooms* but scarcely at all on *schools*.
4 Courses in the history, philosophy, and social foundations of education . . . have seriously eroded.

(Goodlad 1990a: 700–1, original emphasis)

Goodlad concludes: 'the disappointing results we found in the programs we examined are to a considerable degree the legacy of well over a century of neglect' (1990a: 701).

It is only since 1987 that initial teacher education has received serious attention. It is still too early to tell if radical shifts in faculties of education and universities can be achieved, but there are some promising new developments especially in relation to school district–university partnerships (Sirotnik and Goodlad 1988; Watson and Fullan 1991).

In addition to the within-university changes that will be required, changes in school-districts and in schools as workplaces will be essential. Given the teacher education continuum and the fact that teachers spend thirty to thirty-five years as teachers in schools compared to five years in university, the school as a place for teachers to learn or stagnate is crucial. Put another way, classrooms and schools will become more effective when quality people are attracted to teaching and receive effective initial preparation, and the school as a workplace is organized to stimulate and reward accomplishments.

By and large, schools are now not places where teachers can learn to become more effective. We do not need to review the long list of research documenting the individualistic, isolated cultures of schools, which inhibit innovation and teacher improvement (Lortie 1975; Rosenholtz 1989, Fullan and Hargreaves 1991).

We are beginning to see, albeit in the minority, examples of collaborative work cultures which are conducive to continuous teacher development. Rosenholtz (1989) provides a thorough description of thirteen 'moving' or ' learning-enriched' work environments in her study. As she observes, teacher uncertainty (or low sense of efficacy) and threats to self-esteem are recurring themes in teaching (Aston and Webb 1986). In learning-enriched compared with learning-impoverished schools, Rosenholtz (1989: 6) found that teachers and principals collaborated in goal-setting activities (or vision-building) that 'accentuated those instructional objectives toward which teachers should aim their improvement efforts', and that shared goals served to focus efforts and mobilize resources in agreed upon directions. Principals and teacher-leaders actively fostered collegial involvement: 'collective commitment to student learning in collaborative settings directs the definition of leadership toward those colleagues who instruct as well as inspire awakening all sorts of teaching possibilities in others' (Rosenholtz 1989: 68). In effective schools, collaboration is linked with norms and opportunities for continuous improvement and career-long learning: 'It is assumed that improvement in teaching is a collective rather than individual enterprise, and that analysis, evaluation, and experimentation in concert with colleagues are conditions under which teachers improve' (Rosenholtz 1989: 73). As a result teachers are more likely to trust, value, and legitimize sharing expertise, seeking advice, and giving help both inside and outside the school. They are more likely to become better and better teachers on the job: 'All of this means that it is far easier to learn to teach, and to learn to teach better, in some schools than in others' (Rosenholtz 1989: 104).

Becoming better teachers means greater confidence and certainty in deciding on instructional issues and in handling problems. Rosenholtz found that

> Where teachers request from and offer technical assistance to each other, and where school staff enforces consistent standards for student behavior, teachers tend to complain less about students and parents. Further, where teachers collaborate, where they keep parents involved and informed about their children's progress, where teachers and principal work together to consistently enforce standards for student behavior, and where teachers celebrate their achievements through positive feedback from students, parents, principal, colleagues, and their own sense, they collectively tend to believe in a technical culture and their instructional practice.
>
> (Rosenholtz 1989: 137)

Teacher certainty and teacher commitment feed on each other, as Rosenholtz found, increasing teachers' motivation to do even better. All of these factors served to channel energy toward student achievement. Teachers in the learning-enriched schools were less likely to conform to new state or district policies that they judged ill conceived or as directing energies form classroom priorities, and more likely to assess innovations in terms of their actual impact on students.

The development of collaborative work cultures is not straightforward. We ourselves have raised serious questions about superficial and contrived forms of collegiality, as well as the need to respect individuality and individual development (Fullan and Hargreaves 1991). Yet there is no question that we need schools where practices conducive to continuous learning and continuous improvement on the part of teachers become habitual.

The problem of sustained improvement

To start with a discouraging note, neither centralized nor decentralized approaches work. Centralization – intensification being the extreme example – does not work because it attempts to standardize curriculum and performance in a way that is inappropriate and ineffective except for the narrowest goals (Corbett and Wilson 1990; Wise 1988). Decentralization – such as school-based or site-based management – is problematic either because individual schools lack the capacity to manage change or because assessment of attempted changes cannot be tracked. I will start with the problem of school-based models because it is close to providing the conditions for continuous teacher development.

Levine and Eubanks's (1989) research contains an excellent analysis of the problems of local school reform that uses school-based models and empowerment assumptions. They identify six major obstacles:

1 inadequate time, training and technical assistance
2 difficulties of stimulating consideration and adaptation of inconvenient changes

3 unresolved issues involving administrative leadership on the one hand and enhanced power among other participants on the other
4 constraints on teacher participation in decision-making
5 reluctance of administrators at all levels to give up traditional prerogatives
6 restrictions imposed by school board, state and federal regulations and by contracts and agreements with teacher organizations.

(see Levine and Eubanks 1989: 4–8)

Levine and Eubanks turn to the research findings themselves:

As the empowerment movement has coalesced and spread rapidly during the past few years, researchers have begun to assess outcomes in districts which have been early adopters of one or another approach to site-based management and/or enhanced faculty collaboration in decision making. Given the many difficult problems and obstacles such as those enumerated above, perhaps it is no surprise that research-to-date generally has reported conclusions that appear to be more neutral and disappointing than positive and encouraging.

(Levine and Eubanks 1989: 8)

Citing several studies, Levine and Eubanks report that school-based management projects encountered numerous problems over delegation, training and skill requirements, and taking action (see also Lindquist and Mauriel 1989). Ogawa and Malen (1989) in fact, claimed that 'shared governance [in the eight schools they examined] had done more than simply fail to alter traditional decision making relationships; it has actually worked to reaffirm them' by defusing important issues and by developing loyalties without targeted action (1989: 2–3). When positive results were found they tended to be more superficial. David's (1989a; 1989b) study and synthesis of research on school-based management makes this point rather clearly:

In districts that practice school-based management essentials, research studies find a range of positive effects, from increased teacher satisfaction and professionalism to new arrangements and practices within schools. . . . There are [only] a few examples of second-order change, schools that have altered the daily schedule to allow more time for teachers to work together or to increase time devoted to reading . . . This is not surprising, since studies of school improvement find that school councils rarely tackle even instructional issues, let alone second-order change.

(quoted in Levine and Eubanks 1989: 9)

Levine and Eubanks warn us of three dangers. The first problem is 'the confusion between satisfaction and performance'.

There are few if any indications, that early movement toward site-based management has been associated with substantial change in instructional delivery or student performance. To a significant degree, satisfaction may have been attained precisely through neglecting requirements for inconvenient institutional reform [in favour of more superficial easier to implement changes].

(Levine and Eubanks 1989: 20)

The second danger is the 'substitution of site-based management approaches for central responsibilities involving initiation and support of comprehensive school reform efforts' (1989: 20).

If power and resources can be shuffled to the school level, central authorities may also be able to shift most or all of the responsibility for failure to improve student performance to teachers and administrators in the schools . . . It is but one additional small step to treat site-based management as a substitute for district wide reform initiatives.

(Levine and Eubanks 1989: 21)

And the third is 'the confusion between site-based management and "effective schools" approaches' (1989: 24). In particular, Levine and Eubanks emphasize that improvement must focus on instruction: instructional leadership, organization and implementation of instructional services, teacher development, and expectations and monitoring of student performance, which is not necessarily front and centre in school-based management. In other words, restructuring efforts such as site-based management have not yet demonstrated that they focus on, let alone alter, the deeper second-order changes required for reform. The point is not to throw out the baby with the bath-water. Some very significant restructuring efforts involving site-based management are going on, and many more are being developed (David 1989b). The school is still 'the unit of change', but that concept remains one of the most misunderstood in the field of school improvement. Sirotnik (1987) provides a very helpful clarification in his claim that the school should be conceptualized as the *centre* of change. As he states, 'To say that something is at the center implies a good deal around it' (Sirotnik 1987: 21). In his words,

We are led to the organization, eg., the school as the center of change. We are not lead naively to see the school as isolated from its sociopolitical context, able to engage in miraculous self-renewing activities without district, community, state, and federal support. But we are led to where the day-to-day action is, to where with the proper motivation and support, the prevailing conditions and circumstances of schools can be challenged constructively within the context of competing values and human interest . . . In short . . . people who live and work in complex organizations like schools need to be thoroughly involved in their own improvement efforts, assuming significant and enduring organizational change is the purpose we have in mind.

(Sirotnik 1987: 25–6)

A more subtle conclusion is that the school will never become the centre of change if left to its own devices.

There are two broad conclusions that we can draw from this analysis. First, sustained improvement requires serious restructuring of the school, the district, and their interrelationships. The roles of students, teachers, principals, parents, and district staff are all implicated, as is the structure, governance, and design of work and learning (Harvey and Crandall 1988; Elmore 1989; Murphy and Evertson 1990). Schools and districts cannot now manage innovation, and never will be able to without radically redesigning their approach to learning and sustained improvement. Second, and less obvious but equally important, is that schools cannot redesign themselves. The role of the district is crucial. Individual schools can become highly innovative for short periods of time without the district, but they cannot *stay* innovative without district action to establish the conditions for continuous and long-term improvement.

Teacher development at the crossroads

The teaching profession is at the crossroads. There are two dominant contradictory images evident. Cuban (1988) describes these in terms of the teacher as technical actor vs moral actor. The technocrat or bureaucratic image conceives of teachers as giving knowledge and following and applying rules. The moral actor as artisan and craftsperson sees teaching as transforming students. These are ideal types, of course, and it is likely that a mixture of the two is required. There is no denying, however, that in the quest for solutions the teaching profession may find itself being led or going down one road or the other.

We also see the struggle in how collegiality is being pursued. Hargreaves and Dawe (1989) identify two different, contradictory forms of collaboration.

> In the one, it is a tool of teacher empowerment and professional enhancement, bringing colleagues and their expertise together to generate critical yet also practically-grounded reflection on what they do as a basis for wiser, more skilled action. In the other, the breakdown of teacher isolation is a mechanism designed to facilitate the smooth and uncritical adoption of preferred forms of action (new teaching styles) introduced and imposed by experts from elsewhere, in which teachers become technicians rather than professionals exercising discretionary judgment.
>
> (Hargreaves and Dawe 1989: 7)

We see this tension in 'intensification'-based reforms prescribing and assessing teacher competencies vs 'restructuring' efforts to alter the workplace. The implication is that, as with any complex profession, the science and technology of teaching are continually developing, and the job of teaching is an art and science that teachers study, reflect on, and refine throughout their careers (Fullan *et al.* 1990a). I reject the notion underlying many intensification schemes, of the passive professional, but I also rule out the isolated, autonomous professional. *Interactive professionalism* is the notion arising from this analysis. I see teachers and others working in small groups interacting frequently in the course of planning, testing new ideas, attempting to solve different problems, assessing effectiveness, and so on. It is interactive in the sense that giving and receiving advice and help would be the natural order of things. Teachers would be continuous learners in a community of interactive professionals.

Thus the implementation perspective for the future does not simply involve implementing single innovations effectively. It means a radical change in the culture of schools and the conception of teaching as a profession. We have seen glimpses of that future in Rosenholtz's 'learning-enriched' schools, but we have reason to believe that these types of highly energized collaborative schools do not last beyond the tenure of key individuals. By far, the main problem in teaching is not how to get rid of the deadwood, but rather how to motivate good teachers throughout their careers. Changes in the culture of teaching and the culture of schools are required. Cultural change requires strong, persistent efforts because much of current practice is embedded in structures and routines and internalized in individuals, including teachers.

The quality of the teaching force depends on how attractive the profession looks from a distance, and what it is like once you get there. Better compensation, pre-service programmes that link theory and practice in clinical settings, supportive induction programmes, more integrated continuous professional development, opportunities for leadership, and restructuring-type reforms that put teachers in a position to make a difference in the lives of children and adolescents, all contribute to attracting and retaining excellent teachers (Fullan 1991: chs 14 and 15). Intensification-type reforms focusing on narrowly defined and imposed curriculum and teacher competencies repel good people from entering and/or staying. Bureaucratic reforms may be able to guarantee minimal performance, but not excellence in teaching.

The forces reinforcing the status quo are systemic. The current system is held together in many different cross-cutting ways. Achieving improvements will require intensive action of the right kind sustained over many years.

The implementation perspective in the relatively short time period of twenty years has yielded many valuable insights and guidelines for bringing about beneficial changes. It has lead us, however, to move deeper to a more basic set of problems. It is not possible to solve 'the implementation problem' by putting into practice one or more innovations at a time. Substantial progress can be made only by changing roles and organizations, by creating the conditions for people to change how they deal with change.

The legacy of the implementation perspective – largely because it is preoccupied with action and with actual improvement – inevitably has led us beyond into the domain of individual and institutional development. We are now in a position to put innovations and reform themselves into perspective. To see them at best as means to an end and at worst as diversions. As we have clarified the agenda beyond implementation we have also discovered that there is far, far more to bringing about continuous school improvement than hitherto realized.

References

Ashton, P. and Webb, R. (1986) *Making a Difference: Teachers' Sense of Efficacy and Student Achievement*. New York, Longman.

Barth, R. (1990) *Improving Schools from Within: Teachers, Parents and Principals Can Make the Difference*. San Francisco, Jossey-Bass.

Bennis, W. and Nanus, B. (1985) *Leaders*. New York, Harper and Row.

Berman, P. (1981) Toward an implementation paradigm. In R. Lehming and M. Kane (eds) *Improving Schools*. Beverly Hills, CA, Sage.

Berman, P. and McLaughlin, M. (1977) *Federal Programs Supporting Educational Change: Vol VII*. Factors affecting implementation and continuation. Santa Monica, CA, Rand Corporation.

Bird, T. (1986) The mentor's dilemma. Unpublished paper. San Francisco, Far West Laboratory for Educational Research and Development.

Bird, T. and Alspaugh, D. (1986) *1985 Survey of District Coordinators for the California Mentor Teacher Program*. San Francisco, Far West Laboratory for Educational Research.

Block, P. (1987) *The Empowered Manager*. San Francisco, Jossey-Bass.

Carmichael, H. W. *et al.* (1985) *Computers, Children and Classrooms: A Multisite Evaluation of the Creative Use of Microcomputers by Elementary School Children*. Toronto, Ontario Ministry of Education.

Charter, W. and Jones, J. (1973) On the neglect of the independent variable in program evaluation. Occasional paper. Eugene, OR, University of Oregon.

Clark, D., Lotto, S. and Astuto, T. (1984) Effective schools and school improvement: a comparative analysis of two lines of inquiry. *Educational Administration Quarterly*, *20*(3), 41–68.

Coleman, P. and LaRocque, L. (1990) *Struggling To Be Good Enough: Administrative Practice and School District Ethos*. Lewes, Falmer Press.

Corbett, H. D. and Wilson, B. (1990) *Testing, Reform and Rebellion*. Norwood, NY, Ablex.

Crandall, D. *et al.* (1982) *People, Policies and Practice: Examining the Chain of School Improvement, 1–10*. Andover, MA, The Network.

Crandall, D., Eiseman, J. and Louis, K. (1986) Strategic planning issues that bear on the success of school improvement efforts. *Educational Administration Quarterly*, *22*(3), 21–53.

Cuban, L. (1988) *The Managerial Imperative and the Practice of Leadership in Schools.* Albany, NY, State University of New York Press.

David, J. L. (1989a) Synthesis of research on school-based management. *Educational Leadership*, 46(8), 45–53.

David, J. L. (1989b) *Restructuring in Progress: Lessons from Pioneering Districts.* Washington, DC, National Governors' Association.

Elmore, R. F. (1989) Models of restructured schools. Paper presented at the annual meeting of the American Educational Research Association, San Francisco.

Elmore, R. F. (1990) *Restructuring Schools: The Next Generation of Educational Reform.* San Francisco, Jossey-Bass.

Firestone, W. and Corbett, H. D. (1987) Planned organizational change. In N. Boyand (ed.) *Handbook of Research on Educational Administration.* New York, Longman.

Flinders, D. J. (1988) Teacher isolation and the new reform. *Journal of Curriculum and Supervision*, 4(1), 17–29.

Fullan, M. (1985) Change process and strategies at the local level. *Elementary School Journal*, 84(3), 391–420.

Fullan, M. (1988) *What's Worth Fighting for in the Principalship: Strategies for Taking Charge in the Elementary School Principalship.* Toronto, Ontario Public School Teachers' Federation. Also published as *What's Worth Fighting for in Headship?* Buckingham, Open University Press, 1992.

Fullan, M. (1990) Staff development, innovation and institutional development. In B. Joyce (ed.) *Changing School Culture Through Staff Development.* Alexandria, VA, Association for Supervision and Curriculum Development.

Fullan, M. (1991) *The New Meaning of Educational Change.* New York, Teachers' College Press.

Fullan, M. and Hargreaves, A. (1991) *What's Worth Fighting for: Working Together for Your School.* Toronto, Ontario Public School Teachers' Federation. Also published as *What's Worth Fighting for in your School?* Buckingham, Open University Press, 1992.

Fullan, M. and Pomfret, A. (1977) Research on curriculum and instruction implementation. *Review of Educational Research*, 5(47), 335–97.

Fullan, M., Anderson, S. and Newton, E. (1986) *Support Systems For Implementing Curriculum in School Boards.* Toronto, OISE Press and Ontario Government Bookstore.

Fullan, M., Connelly, F. M. and Watson, N. (1990a) *Teacher Education in Ontario: Current Practices and Options for the Future.* Toronto, Ontario Ministry of Colleges and Universities and of Education.

Fullan, M., Miles, M. and Anderson, S. (1988) *Strategies for Implementing Microcomputers in Schools: The Ontario Case.* Toronto, Ontario Ministry of Education.

Fullan, M., Rolheiser-Bennett, C. and Bennett, B. (1990b) Linking classroom and school improvement. *Educational Leadership*, 47(8), 13–19.

Gillis, L. (1985) Field-test report for SHAPE MATE. Unpublished report to the Ontario Ministry of Education, Toronto.

Gillis, L. (1986) Developing software for junior students: good design practices. Unpublished report to the Ontario Ministry of Education, Toronto.

Goodlad, J. I. (1990a) Studying the education of educators: from conception to findings. *Phi Delta Kappan*, 71(9), 698–701.

Goodlad, J. I. (1990b) *Teachers for Our Nation's Schools.* San Francisco, Jossey-Bass.

Goodlad, J. I., Klein, M. *et al.* (1970) *Behind the Classroom Door.* Worthington, Ohio, Charles A. Jones.

Gross, N., Giacquinta, J. and Bernstein, M. (1971) *Implementing Organizational Innovations: A Sociological Analysis of Planned Educational Change.* New York, Basic Books.

Hall, G. E. and Hord, S. (1987) *Change in Schools: Facilitating the Process.* Albany, NY, State University of New York Press.

Hall, G. E., Hord, S. and Griffin, T. (1980) Implementation at the school building-level: the development and analysis of nine mini-case studies. Paper presented at the annual meeting of the American Educational Research Association.

Hargreaves, A. (1989) *Curriculum and Assessment Reform.* Milton Keynes, Open University Press.

Hargreaves, A. (1991) Cultures of teaching. In *Understanding Teacher Development.* London, Cassell.

Hargreaves, A. and Dawe, R. (1989) Coaching as unreflective practice: contrived collegiality or collaborative culture. Paper presented at the annual meeting of the American Educational Research Association, San Francisco.

Harvey, G. and Crandall, D. P. (1988) *A Beginning Look at the What and How of Restructuring.* Andover, MA, The Network, and Regional Laboratory for Educational Improvement of the Northeast and the Islands.

Huberman, M. (1989) Teacher development and instructional mastery. Paper presented at the International Conference on Teaching Development in Toronto, Canada.

Huberman, M. and Miles, M. (1984) *Innovation Up Close.* New York, Plenum.

Jones, L. (1985) A longitudinal study in planned school change. Unpublished doctoral dissertation, University of Toronto.

Joyce, B. and Showers, B. (1988) *Student Achievement through Staff Development.* New York, Longman.

Joyce, B., Murphy, C., Showers, B. and Murphy, J. (1989) School renewal as cultural change. *Educational Leadership,* 47(3), 70–8.

Larter, S. and Fitzgerald, J. (1983) *The Impact of Microcomputers in Elementary Education.* Toronto, Ontario Ministry of Education.

Lee, I. L. (1986) Computer in-service training laboratory teacher evaluations: a partial report of results. Unpublished report.

Leithwood, K. and Jantzi, D. (1990) Transformational leadership: how principals can help reform school culture. Paper presented at the annual meeting of the American Educational Research Association.

Leithwood, K. and Montgomery, D. (1986) *The Principal Profile.* Toronto, OISE Press.

Leithwood, K. and Steinbach, R. (1989a) A comparison of processes used by principals in solving problems individually and in groups. Paper presented at Canadian Association for the Study of Educational Administration annual meeting.

Leithwood, K. and Steinbach, R. (1989b) Characteristics of secondary school principals' problem solving: a comparison with the problem solving of elementary principals and chief education officers. Paper presented at Canadian Association for the Study of Educational Administration annual meeting.

Levine, D. and Eubanks, E. (1989) Site-based management: engine for reform or pipedream? Problems, pitfalls and prerequisites for success in site-based management. Manuscript submitted for publication.

Lindquist, K. and Mauriel, J. (1989) *Useable Knowledge.* New Haven, CT, Yale University Press.

Little, J. (1981) The power of organizational setting. Paper adapted from final report, *School Success and Staff Development.* Washington, DC, National Institute of Education.

Little, J. (1982) Norms of collegiality and experimentation: workplace conditions of school success. *American Educational Research Journal*, 5(19), 325–40.

Little, J. (1987) Teachers as colleagues. In V. Richardson-Koehler (ed.) *Educator's Handbook*. White Plains, NY, Longman.

Little, J. (1989) District policy choices and teachers' professional development opportunities. *Educational Evaluation and Policy Analysis*, 11(2), 165–80.

Little, J. (1990a) The persistence of privacy: autonomy and initiative in teachers' professional relations. *Teachers' College Record*, 91(4), 509–36.

Little, J. (1990b) The mentor phenomenon and the social organization of teaching. In C. Cazden (ed.) *Review of Research in Education 16*. Washington, DC, American Educational Research Association.

Lortie, J. (1975) *School Teacher: A Sociological Study*. Chicago, University of Chicago Press.

Louis, K. (1989) The role of the school district in school improvement. In M. Holmes, K. Leithwood and D. Musella (eds) *Educational Policy for Effective Schools*. Toronto, OISE Press.

Louis, K. and Miles, M. B. (1990) *Improving the Urban High School: What Works and Why*. New York, Teachers' College Press.

Majone, G. and Wildavsky, A. (1978) Implementation as evolution. In H. Freeman (ed.) *Policy Studies Annual Review, II*. Beverly Hills, CA, Sage.

Miles, M. (1986) Research findings on the stages of school improvement. Conference on Planned Change, Ontario Institute for Studies in Education, Toronto.

Mortimore, P., Sammons, P., Stoll, L., Lewis, D. and Ecob, R. (1988) *School Matters: The Junior Years*. Somerset, Open Books.

Murphy, J. and Everston, C. (1990) *Restructuring Schools: Capturing the Phenomena*. New York, Teachers' College Press.

Nias, J., Southworth, G. and Yeomans, R. (1989) *Staff Relationships in the Primary School*. London, Cassell.

Ogawa, R. and Malen, B. (1989) Site-based governance councils: mechanisms for affirming rather than altering traditional decision making relations in schools. Paper presented at the annual meeting of the American Educational Research Association, San Francisco.

Paris, C. (1989) Contexts of curriculum change: conflict and consonance. Paper presented at the annual meeting of the American Educational Research Association, San Francisco.

Patterson, J., Purkey, S. and Parker, J. (1986) *Productive School Systems for a Non-Rational World*. Alexandria, VA, Association for Supervision and Curriculum Development.

Peters, T. (1987) *Thriving on Chaos: Handbook for a Management Revolution*. New York, A. Knopf.

Peterson, K. (1985) Obstacles to learning from experience and principal training. *Urban Review*, 17, 189–200.

Pike, R. (1985) The exemplary lessonware project: a good beginning. Unpublished report to the Ontario Ministry of Education, Toronto.

Pilot School Project (1983) Computers in Ontario. Ontario Ministry of Education, *Review and Evaluation Bulletin*, 4,(5).

Pink, W. (1989) Effective development for urban school improvement. Paper presented at the annual meeting of the American Educational Research Association, San Francisco.

Rosenblum, S. and Louis, K. (1979) *Stability and Change: Innovation in an Educational Context*. Cambridge, MA, ABT Associates.

Rosenholtz, S. (1989) *Teachers' Workplace: The Social Organization of Schools*. New York, Longman.

Ross, J. A. and Reagan, E. M. (1990) Self-reported strategies of experienced and inexperienced curriculum consultants: exploring differences. *Alberta Journal of Educational Research*, *36*(2), 157–80.

Sarason, S. (1971) *The Culture of the School and the Problem of Change*. Boston, MA, Allyn and Bacon.

Sarason, S. B., Davidson, K. S. and Blatt, B. (1986) *The Preparation of Teachers: An Unstudied Problem in Education* (rev. edn). Cambridge, MA, Brookline Books.

Saxl, E., Miles, M. and Lieberman, A. (1990) *Assisting Change in Education (ACE)*. Alexandria, VA, Association for Supervision and Curriculum Development.

Seller, W. and Hannay, L. (1988) The influence of school climate on peer coaching. Paper presented at the annual meeting of the American Educational Research Association, New Orleans.

Sirotnik, K. A. (1987) *The School as the Centre of Change*. (Occasional Paper no. 5). Seattle, WA, Center for Educational Renewal.

Sirotnik, K. A. and Goodlad, J. (eds) (1988) *School–University Partnerships in Action: Concepts, Cases, and Concerns*. New York, Teachers' College Press.

Smith, W. F. and Andrews, R. L. (1989) *Instructional Leadership: How Principals Make a Difference*. Alexandria, VA, Association for Supervision and Curriculum Development.

Smith, L. and Keith, P. (1971) *Anatomy of Educational Innovation: An Organizational Analysis of an Elementary School*. New York, Wiley.

Smylie, M. (1988) The enhancement function of staff development: organizational and psychological antecedents to individual teacher change. *American Educational Research Journal*, *5*(25), 1–30.

Smylie, M. and Denny, J. (1989) Teacher leadership: tensions and ambiguities in organizational perspective. Paper presented at the annual meeting of the American Educational Research Association, San Francisco.

Sparks, D. and Loucks-Horsley, S. (1990) Models of staff development. In *Handbook of Research on Teacher Education*. New York, Macmillan Publishing and the Association of Teacher Educators.

Stallings, J. A. (1989) School achievement effects and staff development: what are some critical factors? Paper presented at the annual meeting of the American Educational Research Association, San Francisco.

Teddlie, C., Kirby, P. C. and Stringfield, S. (1989) Effective versus ineffective schools: observable differences in the classroom. *American Journal of Education*, *97*, 221–36.

Trider, D. and Leithwood, K. (1988) Influences on principal's practices. *Curriculum Inquiry*, *18*(3), 289–311.

Watson, N. and Fullan, M. (1991) Beyond school district–university partnerships. In M. Fullan and A. Hargreaves (eds) *Teacher Development and Educational Change*. New York, Falmer Press.

Wise, A. (1988) The two conflicting trends in school reform: legislative learning revisited. *Phi Delta Kappan*, *69*(5), 328–33.

Yin, R. K. and White, J. L. (1984) *Microcomputer Implementation in Schools*. Washington, DC, COSMOS Corporation.

Yin, R. K., Herald, K. and Vogel, M. (1977) *Tinkering with the System*. Lexington, MA, D. C. Heath.

Index